KU-602-116

TURNER CLASSIC MOVIES BRITISH FILM GUIDES

The Tauris British Film Guide series has, since its launch in 2003, contributed to the revaluation of British cinema by assessing in-depth key British films from the past hundred years. To carry the project forward I.B.Tauris has now entered an exciting and innovative partnership with TCM (Turner Classic Movies), the premier movie channel dedicated to keeping the classic movies alive for fans old and new. With a striking new design and new identity, the series will continue to provide what the *Guardian* has called 'a valuable resource of critical work on the UK's neglected film history'. Each film guide will establish the historical and cinematic context of the film, provide a detailed critical reading and assess the reception and after-life of the production. The series will continue to draw on all genres and all eras, building over time into a wide-ranging library of informed, in-depth books on the films that will comprehensively refute the ill-informed judgement of French director François Truffaut that there was a certain incompatibility between the terms British and cinema. It will demonstrate the variety, creativity, humanity, poetry and mythic power of the best of British cinema in volumes designed to be accessible to film enthusiasts, scholars and students alike.

TCM is the definitive classic movie channel available on cable, satellite and digital terrestrial TV <www.tcmonline.co.uk>.

JEFFREY RICHARDS
General Editor

British Film Guides published and forthcoming:

Whiskey Galore! and The Maggie Colin McArthur
The Charge of the Light Brigade Mark Connelly
Get Carter Steve Chibnall
Dracula Peter Hutchings
The Private Life of Henry VIII Greg Walker
My Beautiful Laundrette Christine Geraghty
Brighton Rock Steve Chibnall
A Hard Day's Night Stephen Glynn
If Paul Sutton
Black Narcissus Sarah Street
The Red Shoes Mark Connelly
Saturday Night and Sunday Morning Anthony Aldgate
A Clockwork Orange I.Q.Hunter
Four Weddings and a Funeral Andrew Spicer

WITHDRAWN FROM STOCK QMUL LIBRARY

PN 1997 · B67 CHI
B765

QM Library

||||||||||||||||||||||||||||||||||||||||||||||||||
23 1287949 8

TURNER CLASSIC MOVIE BRITISH FILM GUIDE
MAIN LIBRARY
QUEEN MARY, UNIVERSITY OF LONDON
Mile End Road, London E1 4NS

DATE DUE FOR RETURN

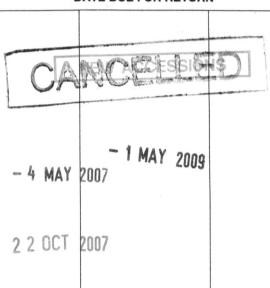

CANCELLED

− 1 MAY 2009

− 4 MAY 2007

2 2 OCT 2007

I.B. TAURIS
LONDON · NEW YORK

Published in 2005 by I.B. Tauris & Co. Ltd
6 Salem Road, London W2 4BU
175 Fifth Avenue, New York NY 10010
www.ibtauris.com

In the United States of America and Canada distributed by Palgrave Macmillan
a division of St Martin's Press, 175 Fifth Avenue, New York NY 10010

Copyright © Steve Chibnall, 2005

The TCM logo and trademark and all related elements are trademarks of and
© Turner Entertainment Networks International Limited. A Time Warner
Company. All Rights Reserved. © and ™ 2005 Turner Entertainment Networks
International Limited.

The right of Steve Chibnall to be identified as the author of this work has
been asserted by him in accordance with the Copyright, Designs and Patents
Act, 1988.

All rights reserved. Except for brief quotations in a review, this book, or any
part thereof, may not be reproduced in any form without permission in writing
from the publisher.

ISBN 1 85043 400 X
EAN 1 85043 400 9

A full CIP record for this book is available from the British Library
A full CIP record for this book is available from the Library of Congress

Library of Congress catalog card: available

Set in Monotype Fournier and Univers Black by Ewan Smith, London
Printed and bound in Great Britain by TJ International Ltd, Padstow, Cornwall

QM LIBRARY
(MILE END)

Contents

Illustrations

Acknowledgements

My thanks go to Peter Graham Scott for doing his best to recall the details of an editing job after more than half a century; to Steve Gamble and John Macintosh for technical support of the highest order; to Pam Barber, Helen Grundy, Frank Gray and James Robertson for unearthing important documentary evidence; to Jeffrey Richards and Philippa Brewster for making this book possible; and to Kara McKechnie for all her help, encouragement and companionship. I am particularly indebted to John Herron at Canal + Images UK for providing generous hospitality on my visit to Pinewood, granting me access to the photographic archive of *Brighton Rock*, and giving permission to reproduce some of its best stills in this book. I must also offer special thanks and acknowledgement to Maire McQueeney for sharing her expertise on *Brighton Rock* with me, allowing me access to her own research materials, providing hospitality in Brighton, and giving me a guided tour of Carlton Hill. To all my friends in Soho-on-Sea I extend my appreciation and confess 'it's been emotional'.

Dedicated to the memory of Graham Greene on the centenary of his birth, and a wonderful Brighton pier – unhappily no more.

Film Credits

BRIGHTON ROCK

American Title	YOUNG SCARFACE
Studios	Welwyn/MGM
Production Company	Associated British Picture Corporation, Charter Films
Director	John Boulting
Producer	Roy Boulting
Associate Producer	Peter De Sarigny
Screenplay	Graham Greene and Terence Rattigan
Shooting Script	Roy Boulting
Novel	Graham Greene
Director of Photography	Harry Waxman (Black/White)
Art Director	John Howell
Editor	Peter Graham Scott
Sound Recordist	Frank McNally
Costumes	Honoria Plesch
Make-up	Bob Clark
Music composed, conducted	Hans May
Song: 'More Than Ever'	Leslie Julian Jones, arranged by John Addison
Production Manager	Gerard Bryant
Assistant Director	Gerry Mitchell
2nd Assistant Director	Guy Wilsdon
3rd Assistant Directors	Cliff Owen, John Redway, Eric Pavitt
Crowd Marshal	George Spence
Continuity	Gladys Reeve
Camera Operator	Gilbert Taylor
Focus Puller	Val Stewart
Clapper Loaders	Bobby Breen, John Harris
Stills	Davis Boulton, W. A. Armour
Assistant Editors	Audrey Bennett, Jean Newsome, Max Benedict
Chief Cutter	Edith Burbeck
Assistant Art Director	Stan Yeomanson

Draughtsman	Don Ashton
Assistant Make-up	Eric Aylott
Hairdresser	Polly Richards
Wardrobe	Hilda Owen
Chief Sound Engineer	Norman Coggs
Boom Operator	Alan Tyner
Dubbing Crew	Harold V. King, Len Shilton
Sound Editor	Audrey Bennett
Stunt Men	Tough Guys Unlimited
Stunt Double (Attenborough)	Christopher Law
Running Time	92 minutes
Length	8,253 ft, 2,517 m
UK Première	8 January 1948
US Première	7 November 1951

CAST

Richard Attenborough	Pinkie Brown
Hermione Baddeley	Ida Arnold
William Hartnell	Dallow
Nigel Stock	Cubitt
Wylie Watson	Spicer
Carol Marsh	Rose
Harcourt Williams	Prewitt
Virginia Winter	Judy
Reginald Purdell	Frank
George Carney	Phil Corkery
Charles Goldner	Colleoni
Alan Wheatley	Fred Hale/'Kolley Kibber'
Lina Barrie	Molly
Joan Sterndale-Bennett	Delia
Harry Ross	Bill Brewer
Campbell Copelin	police inspector
Marianne Stone	waitress
Norman Watson	race-course evangelist
Basil Cunard	[Jim, publican]
Carl Ramon	[Charlie, barman]
Ronald Shiner	[look-out]
Michael Nicholls	[Harold]
Shirley Lorimer	[Shirley]
Wally Patch	[Bill, air gun concession]
Norman Griffiths Orchestra	[orchestra]
Constance Smith	[singer]

Daphne Newton	[manageress]
H. G. Stoker	[registrar]
Anna Steele	[mother superior]
Cyril Chamberlain	[detective]
Michael Brennan	[Crabbe]
Ronnie Head	[Cosmopolitan page]
Billy Bachelor	[Cosmopolitan page]

Other parts played by:
Diana Houlston
Barbara Lott
Philip Godfrey
Tony Halfpenny
Jose Williamson
Jackie Joyner
Diana Maddox

ONE
Filming the Fallen World

The mind is its own place, and in itself
Can make a Heav'n of Hell, a Hell of Heav'n.

(Satan in John Milton's *Paradise Lost*, 1: 254–5)

It is early February 1947 and Britain is in the grip of the worst winter in living memory. As demand for electricity soars, power cuts to domestic users last five hours per day and supplies to many businesses are suspended for days at a time. The BBC closes its television service and the magazines are unable to publish. Film studios are trying to cope by bringing in portable generators. Responding to the well-publicised increase in criminality occasioned by social disruption and commodity shortages, British cinema is in the throes of its first crime cycle. At Isleworth, Harold Huth is working on *Night Beat*. Over at Bushey, Oswald Mitchell is making *Black Memory*. Cavalcanti is shooting *Deep End* (*They Made Me a Fugitive*) at the Riverside Studios. Robert Hamer has just begun making *It Always Rains on Sunday* at Ealing, and David Macdonald, generator permitting, is about to start shooting on *Good Time Girl* at Gainsborough's Shepherd's Bush Studios. At the Alliance Film Studios John Paddy Carstairs and his crew are dressed like polar explorers, as they battle to keep *Dancing with Crime* on schedule. Their star, Richard Attenborough, is under contract to the Boulting brothers, and he is already due to begin work on their new spiv movie at Welwyn Studios. The delay to the availability of their leading player is, perhaps, the least of the Boultings' worries. They are having to secure back-up generators to light sets which await completion because paper hangers are unable to work with frozen paste. The sets, of course, are for *Brighton Rock*. If films contain traces of the conditions in which they are conceived, then the adaptation of Graham Greene's story of a delinquent with a splinter of ice in his heart has a physical as well as a metaphorical resonance. The icicle might have fallen from the studio ceiling.

After cutting their teeth on a few quota-quickies before the war, John and Roy Boulting had established a reputation as innovative independent film-makers, keen to tackle current issues.[1] They had proved themselves capable of handling propaganda subjects in subtle and interesting ways with *Pastor Hall* (1940) and *Thunder Rock* (1942), both directed and edited by Roy and produced by John. Working in the Army and RAF Film Units, they had demonstrated a commitment to social realism in films such as *Desert Victory* (Roy Boulting, 1943) and *Journey Together* (John Boulting, 1945); and, on demobilisation, they were ready to sound a warning to any backsliders in the new Labour administration with their adaptation of Howard Spring's *Fame is the Spur* (Roy Boulting, 1947). The winter of 1947, however, provided a cold coda to the sunny optimism of their wartime short *The Dawn Guard* (Roy Boulting, 1941), in which Bernard Miles famously looks forward to constructing a new Britain:

> There'll be work enough, too, when this lot's over, building up something new and better than what's been destroyed. There mustn't be no more ... dirty, filthy back streets and no more half-starved kids with no room to play in. We got to pack all them up and get moving out into the brightness of the sun. [...] We gotta all pull together.

This was the sort of rhetoric that had helped Clement Attlee's Labour Party to power in the summer of 1945. It projected the vision of a risen nation, liberated from the shackles of poverty and war, striving to realise a dream of social progress – a society of the saved. But this fanfare for altruism and optimism sounded progressively more discordant to an electorate weary of sacrifices and longing for *la dolce vita*.

As the demobbed shivered in their prefabs through the freeze of '47, their power cut, their transportation terminated, their shops starved of stock, Attlee's trumpeting of the spiritual virtues of self-denial must have sounded cracked indeed. It was all a far cry from the New Jerusalem imagined in J. B. Priestley's *They Came to a City* (Basil Dearden, 1944) and, in a Gallup poll, 58 per cent of Britons aged under thirty expressed a desire to emigrate.[2] As the great thaw of March 1947 set in, Bernard Miles's 'dirty, filthy back streets' were submerged under cleansing waters as the country was subjected to floods of biblical proportions. As Harry Hopkins commented: 'Had the British still been followers of the Old Testament they might surely have believed that Jehovah was resolved to chastise them for their lack of humility, their worship of false gods.'[3]

The sense of community and social purpose nurtured during the war was melting away with the snow.

If the nation had found the energy to lift the candle in its bemittened hand and look into the dark mirror of Graham Greene's *Brighton Rock*, it might have seen its condition reflected there. The Brighton Greene had imagined in the economic winter of a decade before was not the city of a risen nation but of a fallen one; not a city of the saved but a realm of the damned. Those who came to *this* city discovered not the New Jerusalem of Priestley's wishful thinking, but a Sodom and Gomorrah of benighted dreams. Like Sartre or Kafka or Eliot, Greene tapped a vein of metaphysical anxiety about a world in which things have fallen apart and make no sense. However, Greene foregrounded a religious dimension of social dislocation and incoherence: the estrangement of the world from its Creator. While all of his novels of the 1930s construct social life as a 'battlefield' of competing interests and ideologies, *Brighton Rock* signals a shift of emphasis from the political towards the spiritual front, in a world which is, for all practical purposes, Lucifer's kingdom. Thus, salvation is the prize of a guerrilla campaign fought at the level of the individual soul and subject to unpredictable tactics and unfathomable judgements. The apparently arbitrary character of divine intervention is a mirror of the administration of secular justice and promotes a common 'terror of life'. This is what gives Greene's fallen world its acute morbidity. In this self-preservation society, people struggle with their own venality, ignorance and weakness, isolated from one another and largely unaware of the political and cosmic forces that circumscribe their dreary and often sordid existence. This is not some temporary state to which Brighton, by some unfortunate mischance, has succumbed; it is the human condition, inescapable on this earth except momentarily in states of ecstatic frenzy occasioned by love or sex or hate. The world, like the human body, is programmed for failure, a state its inhabitants have come to love as much as success.[4] Scobie, the colonial policeman in Greene's *The Heart of the Matter* (written while *Brighton Rock* was filmed), expresses this idea clearly when he wonders why he is so fond of Sierra Leone: 'Is it because here human nature hasn't had time to disguise itself? Nobody here could ever talk about a heaven on earth. Heaven remained rigidly in its proper place on the other side of death, and on this side flourished the injustices, the cruelties, the meannesses, that elsewhere people so cleverly hushed up.'[5]

Brighton, of course, epitomised those places where human suffering was submerged beneath sunny skies and hearty holiday crowds. Pinkie,

1. *A fallen angel in a fallen world: Attenborough as Pinkie. Still from a deleted scene.*

Brighton Rock's youthful gang boss, is in no doubt about the real nature of the life he has experienced at the seaside: 'I'll tell you what life is. It's jail. It's not knowing where to get some money. Worms and cataract, cancer. You hear 'em shrieking from the upper window – children being born. It's dying slowly.'[6]

For most writers, this would be too bleak a vision, but, as Elizabeth Sewell first pointed out, Greene is the inheritor of a tradition of decadent literature that embraces authors such as Poe, Swinburne, Baudelaire and Wilde who were fascinated by the seedy and the sordid.[7] Greene thrives on the dialectic of attraction and repulsion that this fascination evokes, and uses its energy to fuel his heretical hijacking of Catholic doctrine. He finds delight in the paradoxes of faith and morality, a bizarre heroism in sin, and a perverse glamour in the fallen world.

Of course, the fallen world is a persistent theme in both Catholic and Protestant literature and drama, and can trace its lineage back past Milton to Webster and the Jacobean playwrights. Greene particularly admired Webster's ability to express 'the night side of life', with its sense of pessimism and tragedy.[8] Fatalism in tragedy is necessarily related to a view of human nature as fixed and unchanging. The anti-hero of revenge tragedies is ultimately destroyed by the flaws in his character that are evident from the start of the narrative, and *Brighton Rock* was conceived with this template in mind. Although the novel blurs the line between protagonist and antagonist by adopting multiple points of view and attempting to manipulate and disrupt the conventional identifications of its readers, Pinkie remains its central character and spiritual hub. His is the lost soul whose odyssey the book chronicles, and it is his name that describes the colour of the stick of seaside rock (candy) that is the book's prosaic metaphor for the immutability of the human condition. Pinkie is a fallen angel in the fallen world, born in a slum ironically named Paradise Piece, and locked out of heaven by his pride and misanthropy. He represents the sort of dramatic condensation of human experience longed for by Scobie in *The Heart of the Matter*: 'Couldn't we have committed our first major sin at seven, have ruined ourselves for love and hate at ten, have clutched at redemption on a fifteen-year-old deathbed?'[9] Pinkie has struggled out of the 'hell that lay about him in his infancy', led a criminal organisation, committed two murders and attempted to corrupt an immortal soul – all before the eighteenth birthday he will never see.

John Atkins once remarked that Greene 'tries to do for Pinkie what Milton did for Satan'.[10] Through the character of Pinkie, Greene wanted his readers to experience the seductive power of evil evident in the boy's relationship with Rose, a girl from the same hellish slum background who has nevertheless remained good. The similarity in meaning of their names indicates that they represent the dual impulses for good and evil within humanity. Typically, Greene weaves his metaphysical concerns into a thriller driven by the motive power of revenge and the tension between persistence and despair. There are two revengers in the tragedy. The first is Pinkie himself, who sets out not only to avenge the murder of his father figure (the gang boss, Kite), but to exact a more general revenge on life, the great betrayer of hope. The second is Ida, an over-ripe good-time girl with a strong sense of justice, who acts on behalf of Pinkie's first murder victim. While Ida resembles the conventional investigative heroine of detective fiction, Greene uses her to critique the commonsense, secular view of the world that she represents. He contrasts her limited conceptions of right and wrong with a cosmology of good and evil, the everlasting struggle between the eternities of heaven and hell. Ultimately, the pawns involved in this contest are not susceptible to the will of a spirited pagan personality like Ida's, but only to 'the appalling strangeness of the mercy of God'.

Although Greene conceived *Brighton Rock* as a vehicle for the exploration of his religious and political ideas, the book nevertheless offers fertile ground for psychoanalytic interpretation. The author had spent six enjoyable months in the home of a radical Jungian psychiatrist and had undergone dream analysis. It had even been his practice to invent dreams he knew would be highly suitable for psychoanalytic readings.[11] *Brighton Rock* resembles one of those fabrications in the schematic way it dichotomises Brighton into a shallow meretricious overworld and a deep turbulent underworld. The parallel with the conscious and unconscious mind is almost too obvious. Pinkie, too, is a caricature of the ego-driven narcissist, a textbook example of the aggression and violence produced by childhood trauma and sexual repression. His fragile and maladjusted masculinity is constantly challenged by older males, and he lives with a castration anxiety eloquently suggested by the threat of the open razor. Ida, on the other hand, represents the superego, and her maternal sexuality seems designed to reawaken Pinkie's oedipal conflicts. The book is an early example of the tendency, noted by Frank Krutnik, for the noir thriller of the 1940s to be informed by popular psychoanalysis.[12] Mischievously, Greene lays the most tempting of Freudian paper trails, but only to distract attention from the real purposes of his novel.[13]

POST-WAR *NOIR*

> The heavy weight, in post-war British movies, of guilt and gloom, and broodings about crime, is very surprising for a victorious nation busily constructing a kindly Welfare State. (Raymond Durgnat)[14]

Although not fully appreciated at the time of its publication, Greene's *Brighton Rock* is one of the outstanding achievements in twentieth-century British literature. For a film-maker, its relatively simple plot is readily amenable to treatment as a thriller, but the complexities of its philosophical sub-text, and the perversities of its characterisations, present a mighty challenge. At first sight, it seems an unlikely project for the Boultings, whose reputation at the time was founded on the depiction of social rather than metaphysical realities, and who would go on to be known for their acerbic comedies. But *Brighton Rock* is far from being an anomaly in their cinema. Rather, it can be seen as one of a series of their films which discuss the threats posed to the unstable new socialist order of the post-war period, including political backsliding (*Fame is the Spur*), class prejudice (*The Guinea Pig*, 1948) and communist subversion (*High Treason*, 1951). For the Boultings,

Greene's novel dealt with the threat posed by a volatile underclass of individualistic criminals, and the corrosive effects of evil and social deprivation on the young mind. Whereas, for Greene, *Brighton Rock* was about the state of humanity, for the Boultings it was primarily concerned with the state of the nation. However, while Roy and John had not yet embraced the level of cynicism they would display in later pictures, they were far from being the starry-eyed idealists some took them for. Like Greene, they were fascinated by the contradictions of human nature, the messy complexities of reality that undermine the dogma of universal prescription; and in his novel they were shown the 'rock' on which idealism founders. The intractable 'problem' of human nature as a brake on social progress and the play of social forces on the individual became sources of deep fascination for the Boulting brothers.[15] John Hill has also detected in many of the Boultings' films 'a sort of forlorn regret for the fall from grace entailed by the advent of industrialism' that is compatible with *Brighton Rock*'s structure of feeling.[16]

John Boulting once claimed that the brothers made films to please themselves, 'not to please the distributors, nor our critics, nor the public'; but *Brighton Rock* would never have received financial backing from the 'suits' at Associated British and Pathé had it not chimed with emergent imperatives within popular entertainment.[17] By 1946 it was becoming clear to the moneymen of British cinema that the tastes of audiences were fast diverging from those of the wholesome consensus of politicians, social engineers and film critics. The previous year, MOI films adviser, Sidney Bernstein, had published a pamphlet in which he argued that films should portray the positive and attractive side of British society for the international audience. What was required was upbeat optimism – accentuation of the positive – although he recognised that there would be pressure after the war to base dramas around the darker and more sordid aspects of British life.[18] It did not take long for that pressure to exert itself.

The popularity of hard-boiled crime fiction had already been evident before the outbreak of war, both in the sales of imported American pulp magazines and in the adoption of the style by British writers: notably Graham Greene himself with *A Gun for Sale* in 1935. The first prototype noir thrillers were being produced by British film studios, in the face of stringent censorship, from the late 1930s in the form of Soho murder mysteries such as *A Window in London* (1939), and man-on-the-run tales like *They Drive by Night* (1938). The Greene-scripted

The Green Cockatoo eventually saw the light of distribution in 1940, by which time James Hadley Chase's notorious pastiche of an American gangster novel, *No Orchids for Miss Blandish*, was massively outselling more 'respectable' fiction. Like *No Orchids*, *Brighton Rock* had been successfully adapted for the stage, but the stricter censorship regime made both difficult propositions for the cinema. However, the path was cleared early in 1946 by John Harlow's *Appointment with Crime*, a tough gangster thriller in which William Hartnell gave one of the first authentic portrayals of working-class criminality in British films. Its success at the box-office set in motion a cycle of crime films which, controversially, would expose aspects of English life many would have preferred to have kept hidden.[19] Although the film of *Brighton Rock* was first considered by scholars in the 1970s as a literary adaptation, along with other adaptations of Greene's work, it was originally understood primarily as a gangster picture and part of a contemporary cycle. The release of the film coincides, in fact, with the publication of Robert Warshow's seminal article 'The Gangster as Tragic Hero'.[20] Regardless of its setting in the 1930s, contemporary commentators would relate the film to the social concerns of their time. This was perfectly understandable, given its convergence of themes: holiday-making and crime.

BRIGHTON, CRIME AND CINEMA

DAVID: Arsenic, digitalis, belladonna, strychnine; there's enough in that one to kill half Brighton.
PEARL: Just imagine that.

Pink String and Sealing Wax (1945)

During the early post-war years, privation focused desire on those pleasures that were available and affordable, and the cinema and the seaside headed the list. While the chaos in Europe and the expense of foreign travel confined people's holiday horizons, the Holidays with Pay Act (1938) helped in facilitating record numbers of visitors to Britain's newly reopened resorts.[21] Given the enhanced centrality of the coastal resort in British popular culture, it is hardly surprising that the period saw an increasing number of films with a seaside setting. *Holiday Camp* (1947) and *Holidays with Pay* (1949) are indicative of this trend, and the first of these films is also significant in breaking the convention of using the resort purely as a setting for romance and comedy. While the holiday camp of the title remains a place of pleasure-seeking and family entertainment, it is also a venue in which spivs and a sadistic murderer prey on the unwary. Similarly, Blackpool becomes a venue for crime in *Dick Barton Strikes Back* (1949) and *Forbidden* (1949); but Brighton is the resort most closely associated with criminality.

If anything, its reputation is more crucial to the economic well-being of a pleasure resort like Brighton than the sea and the shore. That reputation is formed in the discourse that gives meaning to the town. In Brighton's case, film and fiction have played a significant role. Brighton has enjoyed a long affair with British cinema. It was home to some of its pioneers and, later, to many of its personnel; and has featured in over seventy films. It was even the venue for the wartime speech by Michael Balcon in which he drew his famous distinction between 'realism and tinsel': the genuine and the artificial in films.[22] Both Greene and the Boultings knew Brighton well and, significantly, had enjoyed their first experience of cinema there. Greene had developed a deep attachment to the town after he had been sent to convalesce with an aunt at the age of six, and he returned frequently to recharge his creative batteries. 'No city before the war had such a hold on my affections,' he once confessed.[23] The Boulting brothers had been brought up in respectable Hove where the adjacent town of Brighton was commonly known as 'sin city'.[24]

More than most towns, Brighton has thrived on the contradictions of reputation. Visitors have been drawn by its blend of danger and safety, sophistication and vulgarity, freedom and restraint, the family holiday and the dirty weekend.[25] The town has not been blessed with an unblemished image of moral purity since the patronage of the Prince Regent first overlaid the aroma of fish with the whiff of scandal 200 years ago. From the now lost thriller, *The Brighton Mystery* (1924), films have worked tirelessly to confirm Brighton's special place in the national imagination as a dangerous destination. This representation of Brighton as 'the queen of slaughtering places' is largely the product of a constellation of events, both criminal and literary, occurring during the inter-war years. Clifford Musgrave's *Life in Brighton* points to the influx of well-to-dos and ne'er-do-wells that followed the Zeppelin attacks on London during the First World War. The proximity to wealth and race-course betting encouraged the criminal element to use the town as a base for racketeering, although Musgrave insists that the extent of this activity has been grossly exaggerated.[26] But it was the death and dismemberment of two women in 1934 in what became known as the 'Brighton trunk crimes' that really sealed the association between seaside and homicide. Graham Greene was so obsessed with this grisly 'double event' (in reality very untypical of crime in Brighton during the 1930s) that one biographer has seriously proposed him as a suspect in one of them.[27]

Greene's *Brighton Rock* deepened the connection between Brighton and murder. The book looked beyond Brighton's smiling face to its dark heart, or, to use his own metaphor, 'the shabby secret behind the bright corsage, the deformed breast'.[28] The grand façades of respectable hotels concealed adultery and divorce rackets, and the showy surfaces of the seafront attractions drew attention away from razor slashings and vitriol attacks. Inside the holiday-making Utopia lay a dystopia where a child might be 'violated and buried under the West Pier'.[29] Furious, the *Brighton Gazette* described the book as: 'A gross libel on Brighton which gives a totally wrong and damaging impression of the place and its public officials' implying that it is 'the home of squalid crime, that its hotels are haunted by gangsters'.[30] The paper would not have been any more impressed by the work of local author Patrick Hamilton, already well known for his play about another trunk crime, *Rope*. In 1941, Hamilton published *Hangover Square*, a novel in which homicide seems to be inscribed into the very geography and architecture of the resort:

> While Brighton slept – North Street, West Street, East Street, Western Road, Preston Street, Hove, the hotels, the shops, the restaurants, the movies, the baths, the booths, the churches, the Market, the Post Office, the pubs, the antiques, the second-hand books – slept and gleamed and climbed up from the sea under the dark blue dawn, the enormous gloomy man walked along the front, hardly visible in the darkness, seemingly the only wayfarer, the only one awake. And he looked out at the sea and wondered what it was he had to do. When he remembered he was about opposite the Grand. He remembered without any trouble, any strain. He had to kill Netta Longdon.[31]

Hangover Square was filmed by Twentieth Century-Fox before the end of the Second World War, but commercial considerations persuaded the makers to eliminate the Brighton locations and substitute the Edwardian age for the book's contemporary setting. However, Fox's Hollywood rival, RKO, had no scruples in trading on Brighton's reputation with the evocatively titled *The Brighton Strangler* (1945). John Loder starred as a brain-damaged actor who becomes unable to distinguish real life from the stage play in which he is appearing – with fatal results. Unfortunately, the credibility of the film's fantastical plot is not helped by the

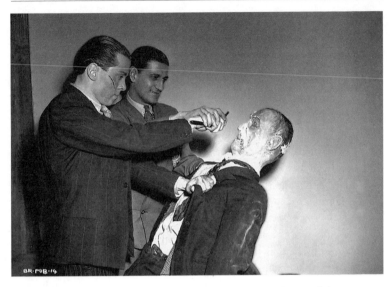

2. *Chiv boys: Carl Ramon instructs Attenborough in the use of the razor.*

attempted simulation of Brighton on standard studio sets. Clearly, neither Max Nosseck nor his art director Albert D'Agostino had ever been to the town or bothered to research its distinctive appearance.

Topographical inaccuracies also abound in an Ealing Studios film set in Brighton which was released almost simultaneously with RKO's chiller. However, Robert Hamer's *Pink String and Sealing Wax* (1945) was based on an actual poisoning case in Brighton in 1871 and takes considerable trouble to get the details of its Victorian setting right. A faithful (if humourless) adaptation of a West End hit by Roland Pertwee, *Pink String* exploits the same period as Patrick Hamilton's *Gaslight* (filmed in 1940) and evokes a similar emotional atmosphere of malevolence to *Hangover Square*, one of Hamer's favourite novels.[32] In contrast to *The Brighton Strangler*'s unalloyed melodramatic excess, *Pink String* uses the melodramatic form to explore the sexual tensions and repression of Victorian England, contrasting the God-fearing gentility of the respectable chemist's household in Regency Square with the gin-fuelled permissiveness of the Dolphin pub. The name given to this house of disrepute, referring as it does to the town's symbol, seems to associate the scene of murder and underworld activity with the town more generally. The association was not missed by the *Evening Standard*'s Patrick Kirwan in his review titled 'There's murder in the seaside air':

Is there something in the Brighton air which so stimulates the human frame that it can only find relief in acts of violence? Or is it that our authors see in its graceful Regency squares, its balconies and bow-fronts, piers and promenade, a background in gentle contrast to the murderous deeds they tell of there? Whatever the reason, Pink String and Sealing Wax does full justice both to the Brighton backgrounds and its tradition of fictional crime.[33]

It demands more than the chemist's (Mervyn Johns) professional expertise to manufacture a *cordon sanitaire* that will protect his family from the libidinous and felonious effects of Brighton's contagious air. As passion erupts into tightly regulated bourgeois lives, the *Pink String* of female desire and the insecure *Sealing Wax* of patriarchal control bind the narratives in a film that is faithful to the spirit, if not the architectural flesh of Brighton. Studio-bound, the film disappointed the anonymous critic of the *News Chronicle* in missing 'golden opportunities of projecting the adorable and unphotographed glories' of the town.[34] The Boulting brothers would try to grab those opportunities in their adaptation of *Brighton Rock*.

GANGLAND

I think I first saw [the Krays] at Brighton with Jack Spot. […] People say that's where the Sabini fight was but they're wrong. It was at Lewes, which got closed down years ago. That's not to say there weren't some good fights at Brighton. There's a free course there as well and that's where a great number of bookies' pitches were; and Spot used to try to organise who stood where and who paid what. Just like the Sabinis did twenty and thirty years earlier. (Frankie Fraser)[35]

As well as being firmly grounded in the authentic milieu of the south coast resort, *Brighton Rock* drew its inspiration from the genuine crime scene of its period. In the early 1930s, off-course cash betting was illegal, but there were more than 14,000 bookmakers operating in Britain; and the increasingly blatant presence of their operatives on the streets of working-class districts caused concern. Designed to ensure a disciplined work force by protecting it against the temptations of gambling, the gaming laws were unpopular and discriminatory. Illicit betting was a £400-million-a-year industry, and inevitably invited the involvement of extortion gangs and corrupt police.[36] The racketeers earned some of their protection money by collecting gambling debts for the bookies,

3. *Young Scarface: Attenborough publicity photo.*

while clerks and tick-tack men doubled as bodyguards. In the south of England, the dominant race-course gang was led by Darby Sabini, the youngest of the six brothers who were the core of a mob with additional business interests in slot machines and Soho clubs. London and Brighton gangster 'Mad' Frankie Fraser worked as a bucket boy for the Sabinis and recalled that they 'ran the bookmakers on the courses in the south of England. If the bookmaker wanted a pitch he had to pay the Sabinis.

They sold him the tissues on which he put up the names of the runners, they sold him the chalk to write the odds, and they had little bucket boys who brought a sponge round to wipe off the odds.'[37]

Sabini was born in 1889 of Irish-Italian parentage in Saffron Hill, London, and, like many British gangsters, took to crime after a failed career as a boxer. But although the Sabinis were physically intimidating, their power was equally dependent on systematic police corruption. Police support was vital in the ongoing conflict with a rival gang based in Birmingham: 'Darby Sabini got in with the Flying Squad [...] the race-course police, the special police, and so they had the police on their side protecting them. Directly there was any fighting it was always the Birmingham mob who got pinched.'[38]

The business was highly lucrative. At Brighton races the Sabinis could expect to make £4–5,000, and at the Derby, four times as much.[39] However, things began to go wrong in 1936 after a cut-throat attack on a member of a rival north London gang, the Whites, at Liverpool Street station. On 8 June, thirty members of White's mob went in search of the Sabinis at Lewes race-course near Brighton, and took revenge on one of their bookmakers, Arthur Solomons, and his clerk. Police intervention resulted in long periods of imprisonment for some of the avengers. The incident would provide the inspiration for the race-course battle in *Brighton Rock*, but it would also mark the beginning of the end for the Sabinis.

By the late 1930s, the East End Jewish gangster Jack 'Spot' Comer was an emerging force, ready to challenge both the Whites and the Sabinis. Working with the race-course mobster Darky Mulley, he developed a system of protection he described as 'an association', to which bookmakers would pay a subscription.[40] The association was powerful enough to prevent displays of violence at race meetings. Darby Sabini's power was eroded first by an ill-conceived libel action against a newspaper that left him bankrupt, and then by his internment at the beginning of the Second World War. He would end his days as a small-time bookmaker in Brighton, dying at his Hove home in 1951. In the meantime, the Whites' criminal empire was gradually eaten away by an alliance of Jack Spot and the robber and racketeer Billy Hill.[41] The endgame came in January 1947 as *Brighton Rock* was in pre-production. Spot attacked Harry White, who was drinking with racehorse trainer Tim O'Sullivan in a club in Sackville Street, and then hid out in a freezing Southend while the police investigated. A pitched battle between the rival mobs at Harringay Arena in April was averted by police intervention, but Spot and Hill finally gained the ascendancy in the second week of July 1947, and control of the race-course at Brighton passed to them just before location filming for *Brighton Rock* moved there.[42] After that, much of the fight had gone out of the Whites and they agreed to settle for control of London's dog tracks with the tacit agreement of the Metropolitan Police. But, before the Boultings' film wrapped, top-dog Billy Hill was on the run in South Africa after his arrest on a robbery charge. By the time *Brighton Rock* was passed by the censor, Hill was in jail, having returned to Britain and given himself up. The film would be released before he was.

TWO
▓▓▓ Planning and Execution ▓▓▓

OFF THE PAGE

My books don't make good films. Film companies think they will, but
they don't. (Graham Greene)[1]

Theatrical rights to Greene's novel had been optioned in January
1939 by one of London's two leading stage production companies,
Linnit and Dunfee. Although originally earmarked for the American
dramatist Sidney Howard, the job of adaptation eventually passed to
Frank Harvey, the author of the hit Linnit and Dunfee play *Saloon Bar*.[2]
Greene had been sent a draft in 1940, but it took three years to bring
the play to the West End, partly because theatre managers feared that
Greene's story would be too depressing for wartime audiences. Bill
Linnit was also convinced that the success of the production would
depend on attracting a big-name actor like John Mills, who could 'open'
the play in the West End. Greene was not convinced. He believed
that Pinkie and Rose should be played by unknowns who could attract
publicity as star discoveries.[3] The problem of a star name, he believed,
could be solved by engaging a well-known music-hall performer to
play the part of Ida. The eventual casting conformed partly to these
ideas, but that did not mean that Greene was pleased. Nineteen-year-old
Richard Attenborough, fresh out of bomb-damaged RADA, was cast
as Pinkie, while his Rose was to be played by the promising young
actress Dulcie Gray. Linnit found a name he could put above the title
in Hermione Baddeley, who took the role of Ida.

Greene eventually approved the script in January 1943, shortly
before the play opened its provincial run in Blackpool, although he
could not agree to the attempt to soften the ending. As he told his
wife and his agent:

I must insist on the ending being kept. Linnit had some crazy idea of
getting Rose to consent 'to be looked after by Ida' – which means that

he's lost the point of the whole thing as Ida is the real villain of the piece and Harvey has brought that out quite well. [...] The last part of the book did more than anything else to get it under people's skin, and so it will be in the play. It's a magnificent curtain.[4]

The ending of *Brighton Rock* – 'the worst horror of all' – was described by Marghanita Laski as 'the most memorable, most painful any novelist has ever written', and would remain a contentious issue for adaptors.[5] Greene policed it from the very start. His worst fears were confirmed when, returning from his intelligence posting to Sierra Leone, he caught a performance of the play at the New Theatre, Oxford. He found that the crucial final scene was missing, and that Ida had been turned into the heroine of the piece. Convinced that Linnit was responsible for the changes, Greene snubbed him after the performance and threatened that, unless the revisions to his story were withdrawn, the name of Graham Greene must be removed from all publicity. He was quickly given assurances that every effort would be made to carry out his wishes for the play's London opening at the Garrick Theatre the following week. Some last-minute changes may have been made, but surviving evidence suggests that the epilogue, in which a priest discusses the 'appalling strangeness of the mercy of God' and the unsuspecting Rose waits by the gramophone to play Pinkie's message of hate, was not reinstated for the West End run.[6] Angry as he was, Greene probably lacked the time and energy to enforce his threats and settled for the financial returns brought by a West End hit. He had thought the production poorly directed (by Richard Bird) and 'extraordinarily careless', and believed that Baddeley was crude and grotesque in her role.[7] Audiences generally thought differently, giving her 'round after round of applause for ensuring that virtue triumphs over vice'.[8] This would only have added insult to injury for Greene, who saw the meaning of his text diminished into a conflict between right and wrong instead of a battle between good and evil.[9] Greene, however, was on the same wavelength as audiences and critics in praising many of the performances, including Harcourt Williams as Prewitt, and Attenborough, whom he described as 'a most promising young actor'.[10]

The popular success of *Brighton Rock* on stage confirmed its potential as a film, but reports of its imminent transfer to the screen had been in circulation within a few weeks of the novel's publication. On 24 September 1938, the *Brighton and Hove Herald* reported: 'The screen rights to *Brighton Rock* have been sold and production is expected to start shortly at British Lion Studios. Graham Greene has agreed to collaborate on the script.' There is no corroboration of the sale, and the buyer is not named but, at the time, the financially stretched British Lion company was leasing its Beaconsfield studios to Herbert Wilcox and George King. Certainly, the film rights were eventually optioned by a consortium of Bill Linnit, Terence Rattigan, Anthony Asquith and Tolly de Grunwald, but if the *Herald* report is accurate, they cannot have been the initial buyers, as their collaboration did not begin until early in 1939.[11] However, the memorandum of agreement drawn up when the consortium came to sell the rights clearly indicates that they were purchased from Graham Greene (rather than a third party) on 28 January 1939.[12]

A certain amount of confusion also surrounds the acquisition of the rights by the Boultings. The twins had been interested in the rights ever since they had followed the serialisation of Greene's novel in the *Evening Standard* in 1939.[13] Lord Attenborough certainly remembers discussing the project with them before the end of the Second World War: 'During this period, the man who was my immediate commanding officer was John, and he and Roy both started talking about the possibility of a film. They had seen *Brighton Rock* on the stage, and they said to me, "Look, this is something we want to do as a major movie".'[14]

Word of this may have reached the consortium because, shortly before the end of the war, the Boultings received a call from the consortium's literary agent, Robert Fenn. As Roy Boulting recalled:

> Fenn, who we knew and respected, told us that his three clients, all experienced film-makers, had been working hard trying to turn the book into a screenplay, without success. Knowing our admiration for Greene as a writer, Fenn asked us if we would be interested enough to pick it up and take it off their hands. Well we were, we did, and the film rights became ours.[15]

But it was not quite as simple as that. Negotiations over the sale were protracted, with de Grunwald (described by the Boultings as the Svengali to Rattigan and Asquith's Trilby), at one point, reluctant to relinquish control.[16] Nor were Rattigan and Asquith content to abandon all interest in the project. Asquith continued to be the director designate of the picture until a few weeks before principal photography began, and Rattigan was happy to earn a fee by writing a screenplay. John Boulting had already collaborated with Rattigan on *Journey Together* for the RAF Film Unit; but, unconvinced that he was the best writer for this particular subject, was keen to persuade the original author to adapt his novel. Initially reluctant following some painful experiences with scriptwriting in the late 1930s, Green was persuaded by the twins, who 'were delighted to the point of smugness'.[17] Rattigan agreed to collaborate with Greene and to share the £6,000 fee. The deal was not completed until the first week of 1947. By that time, the Boultings had struck a further deal with the vertically integrated Associated British Picture Corporation to finance and distribute the picture. ABPC, part-owned by the American major Warner Bros, was second only to the Rank Organisation as a force in post-war British cinema. It would become notorious in later years for its parsimonious budgets, but, in the euphoria generated by returning to production after a long war, *Brighton Rock* was given a generous allocation: £178,000, at the high end of the medium budget range. It was almost ten times as much as a supporting feature could expect, but less than a colour film might command, and only half of the money the more lavish Rank Organisation would spend on its most prestigious productions.[18] It was still a lot of cash for a gangster movie. ABPC clearly saw the Boultings as safe pairs of hands and *Brighton Rock* as a sound commercial proposition. As the company's flagship studio at Elstree was still not ready after requisition by the Royal Ordnance Corps during the war, *Brighton Rock* was booked into ABPC's smaller second studio at Welwyn, which had remained open for the duration. Not yet subject to the iron financial control ABPC's head of production Robert Clark would soon exercise, the Boultings enjoyed considerable freedom and a positively profligate shooting schedule stretching over half a year.

THE SCREENPLAY

The battle of heaven and hell cannot be convincingly conveyed in a mode of humdrum everyday realism ... The wild and bloody conventions of Elizabethan melodrama provided a most appropriate vehicle for conveying his hell-haunted vision of human existence. (Lord David Cecil on John Webster in *Poets and Story-tellers*, 1949)

When the Boultings bought the rights to Graham Greene's novel for £12,000, they also bought the rights to Frank Harvey's stage adaptation.[19] The importance of this should not be underestimated, because the way in which the stage play concentrated events into a small number of locations – in particular the Palace Pier – would be significant in the construction of the screenplay. In their obituary for Frank Harvey in *The Times*, the twins made it clear that they considered his adaptation of *Brighton Rock* 'brilliant', and they must have indicated to Greene that some of the revisions Harvey had introduced would be beneficial to the cinematic realisation of the text. It was Rattigan, however, who was charged with producing the first film treatment – based on Greene's novel rather than Harvey's play – which he rushed to complete in a few weeks. On 24 August 1946 Rattigan sent his fifty-three-page treatment to John Boulting with the following comment:

> You should never have asked me and I should never have agreed to do the treatment in so short a time. However, I refuse to make excuses and, provided the enclosed is not taken as conclusive, I feel that it may well provide a useful basis for discussion.
>
> I have taken you at your word and not bothered about Mr. Breen. Obviously in later scripts you will have to make him a few more concessions than I have done in this, but for the purpose of this treatment I have assumed that the censorship problem is no more acute than would normally be provided by the Lord Chamberlain for a play.
>
> I have altered Graham Greene's construction a fair amount – less at the beginning than at the end – where I feel the tempo of the physical action slows from the film point of view disastrously. I have also invented my own murder. These and other alterations I have made I trust you will forgive.[20]

There are two things here that are worthy of comment. First, the Mr Breen whose censorious requirements would have to be accommodated was not the Secretary of the British Board of Film Censors, but the leading administrator of the more draconian American Motion Picture Production Code. This is revealing of the covert influence of American censorship practices on a British film industry charged with the need to export its products to the largest market in the world. Second, although Rattigan implies that his treatment offers some radical revisions and innovations, it actually took few liberties with either narrative or characterisation. Changes are generally of detail rather than structure:

1. Fred is killed on the Dante's Inferno ride.
2. Pinkie attempts to 'carve' Corkery at his home, but is intercepted by the police.
3. The conversation at Prewitt's home is with Ida rather than Pinkie.
4. Towards the end of the narrative, a suspense scene is introduced

between Ida and Cubitt on the Dante's Inferno ride, where he tries unsuccessfully to dispose of her in the same way that Fred had been killed. This is presumably what Rattigan meant when he wrote that he had invented a murder of his own.

5. Most significantly, the final scene is set in Corkery's villa where a traumatised Rose has been looked after by Ida since Pinkie's death. Here she is spared 'the worst horror of all' by damage to the record of Pinkie's voice.

While Greene might have objected that *Brighton Rock* was too 'proletarian' a subject for Anthony Asquith, he generally admired Asquith as a director. His respect for Rattigan's writing was much more grudging. His review of the duo's collaboration on *French without Tears* (1939) had described it as a 'triumph' for Asquith's 'witty direction and firm handling of the cast' over 'the too British sexuality of Mr Rattigan's farce'.[21] Rattigan was affronted by Greene's review and the omens for a fruitful collaboration were never good.[22] Greene's response to Rattigan's treatment was dismissive, as he recalled over twenty years later: 'Terence Rattigan wrote a treatment of a few pages with quite a different ending which was not used: the script was not really a collaboration.'[23] In 1984 Greene was still peddling the same account: 'He had done a treatment with a happy ending. I can't remember how happy it was. It was *very* happy. In fact I did the whole screenplay myself. He didn't contribute anything.'[24] But Greene was being typically disingenuous. While he had rejected most of Rattigan's revisions, especially the idea that Ida and Corkery might look after Pinkie's widow, he was struck by the idea of the message of hate sticking and sparing Rose's feelings. As Attenborough once correctly remarked, 'that was Terry'.[25] The idea resonated with something Greene had written in an essay entitled 'Film Lunch', at the time he was working on *Brighton Rock*. He had used the occasion of a lunch held to celebrate MGM's decision to produce films in Britain to launch an attack on the banality of Hollywood scriptwriting. Writers, it seemed, were rewarded for 'forgetting how people live' and churning out dialogue like '"I love, I love" endlessly repeated'.[26] The irony of ending his script for *Brighton Rock* in just this way and pocketing £3,000 must have been irresistible. And he certainly wasn't going to allow Rattigan to take the credit.

Rattigan having delivered his treatment, the ball was now in Greene's court. At the time, Greene had reached a hiatus in his writing career before beginning *The Heart of the Matter*. He was working as the com-

4. *Little girl lost: The deleted railway station sequence with Lina Barrie,
Joan Sterndale-Bennett, and Harry Waxman's daughter, Sally.*

missioning editor for Eyre and Spottiswoode, introducing a fashionable
new line of Soho thrillers by authors such as Edgar Lustgarten and
James Hadley Chase. As well as the demands of his day job, Greene's
time was further limited by the complexities of his love life. Already
managing a marriage and a long-term affair, he added the complication

of a new relationship with Catherine Walston, the American wife of a British landowner.

Greene initially responded to Rattigan's respectful adaptation of his novel with a much more radical approach of his own. He thought the film might benefit from an earlier and more intense focus on Rose, allowing the exploration of the social conditions from which both she and Pinkie had emerged. His treatment begins in Rose's slum home at Nelson Place. She has just packed her suitcase in preparation for her residency at Snow's Restaurant and is saying farewell to her mother. Geographically, the journey may be only half a mile, but, socially, Snow's is a world away and she must leave home to live at her place of work. Her father sits sullenly, refusing to say goodbye. Defeated by circumstance, he represents exactly what Pinkie is trying to escape by adopting a life of crime. We follow Rose as she makes her way past a demolition site to the edge of the slum clearance area where she pauses at the 'frontier between two worlds' as she looks back and then forward towards 'the sea, the front, the glitter'. The camera moves rapidly with Rose as she almost runs into 'this cheerful, lavish, spendthrift Brighton' which is preparing itself for a Whitsun with a fine weather forecast. She passes posters advertising the arrival of the *Daily Messenger*'s mystery man, Kolley Kibber, before knocking on the door of Snow's, where she is greeted and shown to the room she will share with Doris. Clearly, Greene wanted to stress the sense of excitement and liberation she feels. As she stares into the first full-length mirror she has ever seen, 'as a man might stare into a crystal to see the future', we hear her thoughts: 'This is life, this is. Things are going to happen from now on.' But what happens immediately is that her excited breathing forms a mist on the mirror and her face is obscured. When the mist clears we are at Brighton station witnessing the arrival of Kolley Kibber, who makes his way to the Feathers.[27]

This early fragment of a treatment (it runs to only fourteen pages and breaks off after Fred's murder) is important for what it indicates about Greene's thinking on the appropriate way to adapt his novel. First, it lays emphasis on the social contrasts within the story's setting: the two Brightons, the one cheek by jowl with the other. Second, it attempts to balance out the preoccupation with Pinkie by ensuring that at least one character will have an existence independent of her relationship to him. Third, it attempts to realise Greene's theories on the value of a poetic cinema, constructed around fidelity to people's lived experience and the juxtaposing of powerful images that speak of what is, what is thought to be, and what ought to be. The insight into life at Nelson Place, the pausing of Rose at the junction between two worlds, and the dissolving of her aspirations in the misted mirror, are all examples of the building blocks that might be used to construct such a 'simple, sensuous and passionate' poetic cinema.[28] For such a cinema of 'personal lyric utterance' to be popular, however, Greene appreciated that it had to excite audiences, as the dramas of the Elizabethan stage had done. Only then might one be able to communicate 'what you will of horror, suffering, truth'.[29] That this was easier in theory than in practice was evidenced by John Boulting's response to Greene's left-field approach to the opening of his *Brighton Rock* film treatment. On 21 October 1946 Boulting forwarded Greene's effort to Terence Rattigan, and tried to set up a meeting with Greene at Rule's restaurant, commenting that neither Greene nor himself was 'altogether happy' with the treatment, and that both would value Rattigan's opinion. Boulting's difficulties with the treatment were twofold: 'It seems to me that we are now taking too long to get to the death of Hale, and it would also seem to me that it would be inadvisable to open the film on Rose – although the squalid background has certainly some value – if we are obliged to lose her almost immediately for a not inconsiderable period.'[30]

Boulting's desire to get quickly to the murder of Hale reveals that he, like Rattigan, conceived the film primarily as a thriller rather than a drama of characters and ideas. This was the way Harvey's stage adaptation had approached it, and this had clearly proved popular with the paying public. Mindful of the need to supply their financial backers ABPC with a viable entertainment product, the Boultings were keen to stress the entertainment value of their film. As John told a visiting trade journalist during filming: 'There will be plenty of movement with action, thrills, suspense and, despite an apparently sombre atmosphere, some moments to provide laughter.'[31] For Greene, the elements of the thriller provided the means of engaging an audience who could then be exposed to the profundities of 'horror, suffering, truth'. Broadly, then, the issue was whether the thriller was a means to an end or an end in itself. However, although the book's social and religious themes and its complex moral discourses attracted differing levels of commitment, what all parties could agree upon was the need to ground the action of the thriller in an authentic and convincing setting. In his film criticism, Greene had consistently praised films he found to have a convincing *mise-en-scène*. For him, this was the potential advantage film had over theatre: '[Film] because it can note with more exactitude and vividness than the prose of most living playwrights the atmosphere of mean streets and cheap lodgings, gives the story background and authenticity. We recognise the truth of the general scene and are more prepared to accept the truth of the individual drama.'[32] The flowering of social realism in British cinema during the Second World War had set new standards for film-makers, but even before the opening of hostilities, Arthur Woods had pointed the way towards a convincing depiction of a low-life milieu with *They Drive by Night*. Greene's admiration for this adaptation of James Curtis's novel about a man on the run is evident in his review:

> [S]et against an authentic background of dance palaces, public houses, seedy Soho clubs, and the huge wet expanse of the Great North Road, with its bungaloid cafes, the grinding gears, the monstrous six wheeled lorries plunging through the rain, [the] film has taken characters in a simple melodramatic situation and given them a chance to show with some intensity their private battlefields.[33]

The film of *Brighton Rock* would mix melodrama with authenticity in a similar way, because, in Greene's philosophy, the two were not incompatible. Genuine emotional melodrama was the tried-and-tested carrier of truths about good and evil. On this Greene was at one with the Boultings, who were not averse to using melodrama in their passionate pursuit of cinematic realism.

His attempt to shift the narrative's emphasis more towards Rose having been rejected, Greene worked through November on a more conventional treatment, trying to adapt his favoured technique of moving between the viewpoints of different characters. On film, their internal monologues had somehow to be externalised, either through dialogue, voiceover or point-of-view shot. The omniscience of the literary narrator was not possible for the camera. As Greene realised, it was inevitable that something would be lost.[34] He was also acutely aware of the problems of turning a melancholic novel like *Brighton Rock* into an entertainment acceptable to Associated British. While working on his book ten years before, he had remarked on the almost insoluble difficulties of filming Conrad's *Secret Agent*, lamenting that such a 'dark drab passionate tale of Edwardian London could never find a place in the popular cinema'; its qualities of 'madness and despair' were simply not suited to the business of mass entertainment.[35] Not that Greene was opposed to popularity. 'Films have got to appeal to a large undiscriminating public,' he had written, 'a film with a severely

5. *A visit from the author: John Boulting with Graham Greene (centre) and Nigel Stock on the set at Welwyn.*

limited appeal must be – to that extent – a bad film.'[36] But the kind of cinema he wanted to create would eschew a path to popularity paved in soothing, muted inoffensiveness, in favour of one lined with honest vulgarity and dramatic tension. Greene always maintained that he was granted almost total autonomy in the development of what amounted to a shooting script:

> The Boulting Brothers gave me too much rope and they asked a bit too much in a way. They asked for almost a shooting script and a writer is not really capable of doing a shooting script – it's a waste of time. [...] And so it was rather a fatigue doing it and I saw very little of the Boulting Brothers, but simply sent my pages along to them.[37]

The Boultings may have given plenty of latitude to a writer they greatly admired; but they knew better than to entrust a shooting script to someone who might have a sound grasp of what would make effective cinema, but who had not been through the processes of training and apprenticeship experienced by most professional film-makers. They probably subscribed to the dominant industry view that a practical knowledge of editing was an important prerequisite for the production of a final screenplay. They were, however, delighted with what Greene gave them to work with, as Roy Boulting confirmed: 'What he eventually came up with may have been a trifle "rough" as a final screenplay; but it was all that we had hoped for, containing, as it did, the distilled essence of a story that was pure "film" from beginning to end.'[38] Conscious of the potential disapproval of the Catholic Church and the consequences for Greene personally and the film commercially, his script was submitted to the Dominican theologian Father Gervase Matthew. His response was favourable: 'I admire your treatment greatly. In my opinion it contains nothing that is in any way offensive either to Catholic faith or morals. I know of no better exposition of the Catholic doctrine of the nature of sin.'[39]

The copy of the shooting script held in the British Library attributes it to Roy Boulting, who worked on it during a protracted stay in Brighton in the first weeks of 1947. He recalled:

> In search of locations backgrounds, I traipsed up and down the Palace Pier and across the pebble beaches; discovered the dramatic web of narrow lanes between the clocktower and the sea front; scoured the sleazy area around Brighton's Kemp Town; found those pubs the race gangs had haunted on the eve of a meeting; trudged up on to the Downs to take pictures of the racetrack [...] At the end of a month, I sat down to incorporate all this detailed research into Graham's screenplay. Two weeks later, the final work had been broken down loosely into shots. I returned to London and handed over the blueprint – the shooting script – to brother John. [...] Generously, no objection was raised to Terry's name appearing up on the screen credits; but adaptation and writing glory were, in truth, entirely Graham Greene's.[40]

During his Brighton visit, Boulting met a card sharp and ex-member of the Sabini gang, Carl Ramon, whom he engaged as an actor and consultant for the film: 'He was a brilliant find, and he helped Dickie [Attenborough] learn how to speak, walk and wear his clothes correctly.'[41] Ramon's recruitment was testimony to the commitment to authenticity that set the Boultings apart from most of their contemporaries. '[F]rom the beginning of our filmmaking,' Roy once commented, 'John and I sought to convey, in subject or technique, or both, a feeling for the truth. We shied away from the trite escapism to which pre-war British films had been wedded.'[42]

With their film waiting to go finally into production, the Boultings nervously submitted their script to the BBFC. The Board's comments at scenario stage were a vital insurance against the costly filming of material that might later prove unacceptable to the censor. The

6. *The biggest set in Britain: Val Stewart (focus puller), Gilbert Taylor
(operator), and John Boulting aboard the crane at MGM Elstree.*

naturally conservative Board was known to be at its most defensive
where indigenous gangster narratives were concerned. In the previous
decade the Board had nipped similar projects in the bud before production, but there had been signs just before the war that its attitudes
were beginning to soften.[43] After a wartime hiatus the Board had been
suddenly faced with a resurgent genre, stimulated by the fashion for
hard-boiled crime fiction and noir thematics. Early in 1946 it had
received a scenario for what would become *Appointment with Crime*, an
unprecedented and fairly uncompromising study of revenge within the
London underworld. It would star William Hartnell, soon to be one of
the leading players in the Boultings' film. The BBFC's response had
been to trim some of *Appointment*'s more graphic displays of violence
and surgery, but reluctantly to allow the theme and narrative to pass
unmolested into production.[44] In hot pursuit of *Appointment*'s success,
Alliance Films had submitted scenarios for *Dancing with Crime* (as *South
East Five*) and *They Made Me a Fugitive* (as *A Convict Has Escaped*),
two more stories presenting disturbingly realistic pictures of organised
crime in the capital. *Dancing with Crime*, which would star *Brighton Rock*'s
Richard Attenborough, certainly possessed socially redeeming features
in the way elements of the community turned on exploitative criminals,

but *They Made Me a Fugitive* was a more direct challenge to prevailing regimes of taste and morality. The censor had engaged in some wringing of hands, but eventually agreed to allow the film on condition that some of its violence was toned down, commenting: 'This type of film is not to be encouraged as in my opinion it is far too sordid, but I cannot see on what grounds we can turn it down.'[45] Under protest, the green light had effectively been given to *Brighton Rock*, and its passage through the choppy waters of censorship was likely to be eased slightly by its literary credentials and the Boultings' reputations as serious and socially-conscious film-makers. One concern of BBFC examiner Madge Kitchener about *Fugitive*, however, would have repercussions for the Boultings' film. She was disturbed by the use of religious quotation in such a sordid context and, when the *Brighton Rock* scenario was considered, this became a significant issue. Pinkie's quotations from the Catholic Mass, which had caused hardly a twitch from Father Matthew's eyebrows, created consternation in the Board. They had to go, and with them went much of the film's theology. The violent application of razor blades and vitriol was also deemed unacceptable, but the story, with its exposure of evil and its moral and wholesome ending, was passed.

The Boultings must have been relieved. It was common practice in the days of strict censorship to offer the Board a scenario with gratuitous material to cut, in the hope that other questionable but more essential elements might escape the blue pencil. Religious quotation and vitriol they could manage without, but the prohibition on razor blades posed more of a problem, as these were the tools of Pinkie's trade, and the razor-scarred cheek was the emblem of his profession. The Boultings' response was to change Pinkie's weapon-of-choice from a (temptingly imitable) blade taped to the fingernail to a (more conventional and dramatic) taped cut-throat razor, and to hope that the censor would appreciate the impossibility of having a razor gang without any blades. They were in luck, and the Board passed the finished film uncut on 23 September 1947.

As a film critic, Greene had been outspoken in his questioning of censorship practices in the 1930s. He had publicly expressed his resentment of the dead hand of the BBFC when it came to trying to portray anything resembling excitement or honest vulgarity on the screen, and the consequent retreat of film-makers towards the bourgeois refinement of the popular novel and West End play.[46] He might have anticipated an attempt to prohibit vitriol and razors, but the excising of religious quotations in Latin exasperated him. 'Apparently,' he wrote in an irate letter to the *Daily Mirror* after *Brighton Rock*'s release, 'one is allowed a certain latitude in using the name of God as an expletive, but any serious quotation from the Bible is not permissible on the English screen.'[47]

CAST AND CREW

I'm the only one in this mob who knows how to act. (Pinkie in *Brighton Rock*)

Richard Attenborough (Pinkie) Now one of the best-known public figures in Britain, Lord Attenborough was born in Cambridge in 1923 and educated in Leicester where his father was principal of the University College. He acted in his first film while still at RADA, thanks to a repertory performance seen by his future agent Al Parker, who then secured a breakthrough role for him as the cowardly young stoker in *In Which We Serve* (1942). While making this film he first met the Boultings, who were filming *Thunder Rock* on the next stage at Denham. Attenborough walked out of RADA into a string of roles in London's theatreland, and the lead in the stage production of *Brighton Rock*. There was never much doubt that he would take the role to the screen when he joined the RAF Film Unit and, under the direction of John Boulting, played a trainee pilot in *Journey Together*. After the war, Attenborough managed to come out smelling of roses from an otherwise malodorous screen adaptation of another Graham Greene novel, *The Man Within* (1947). Now under contract to his close friends the Boultings, he managed to fit in a leading role as a combative taxi driver in *Dancing with Crime* while *Brighton Rock* was in pre-production. At the age of twenty-four, Attenborough would follow up his triumph in *Brighton Rock* by playing a schoolboy in the Boultings' next film *The Guinea Pig* (1948). He would star in a further forty films before playing another psychotic murderer in *Ten Rillington Place* (1970). By that time, he had also established himself as a producer and director. *Gandhi*, the story he had laboured to bring to the screen for almost twenty years, would bring a clutch of Academy Awards in 1982, and they would be followed by an avalanche of distinctions over the following two decades. As an octogenarian, the Boultings' Pinkie remains as perky as ever.

Hermione Baddeley (Ida) The indefatigable Hermione Baddeley made her debut on the London stage in 1919 at the age of twelve, and her

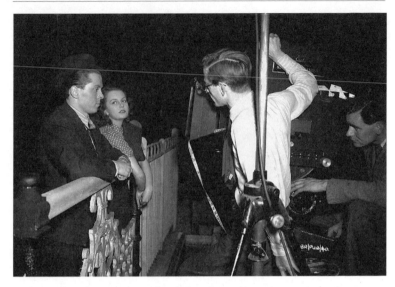

7. *Taking direction: Attenborough and Carol Marsh on set at Welwyn with John Boulting.*

flair for comedy and satire soon established her as a top revue artiste during the 1920s and 1930s. She had made her screen debut at the end of the silent era, but had accepted only a handful of film offers before the Boultings persuaded her to reprise her stage role as the down-to-earth Spiritualist revenger Ida Arnold in their screen version of Greene's book. It would prove a turning point in her career and she would go on to appear in more than thirty films in the twenty years following *Brighton Rock*'s release. Baddeley went to live in Brighton's Kemp Town at the end of the 1950s. She died in 1986.

Carol Marsh (Rose) The long search to find the Boultings' perfect Rose ended with seventeen-year-old Norma Simpson, the daughter of a London architect and a freshly enrolled student at the Rank 'Charm School'. Like Rose, Norma had enjoyed a Catholic education, in her case at the Convent of the Sacred Heart in Hammersmith, where she had shown considerable promise as a singer. It was a surprise to every-one when she made acting her career. When she auditioned for the Boultings, however, they were in no doubt that she had considerable talent as an actress and just the air of innocence they were looking for in their ingenue. Norma was quickly renamed Carol Marsh (Marsh was her mother's maiden name) and groomed for stardom. But stardom for

Carol was to be elusive. After *Brighton Rock* she was given a leading role in *Helter Skelter* (1949), a madcap comedy in which she played a girl with persistent hiccups, and the title role in *Alice in Wonderland* (1951), a French interpretation in which most of the parts were played by puppets. There was a handful of supporting roles for Carol during the 1950s – the most famous was as Lucy in Hammer's *Dracula* (1958) – but her film career had stalled by the end of the decade. She did continue to work in the theatre, on radio and has clocked up more than 300 television appearances. She is one of the few survivors among the cast of *Brighton Rock*.

William Hartnell (Dallow) Now immortalised as the first Dr Who, William Hartnell began his stage career in comedy roles before becoming a regular face in the British quota films of the 1930s. The work was irregular, until he landed a substantial role in a Nettleford Studios' 'quickie', *I'm an Explosive* (1933). When comedy roles began to dry up, Hartnell decided to rebrand himself as a tough guy, studying criminology and researching in dance halls and dives. At the outbreak of the Second World War, he joined the Tank Corps, but was soon invalided out. Consequently, he was able to appear in some of the quintessential social realist films of the war, including *The Bells Go Down* (1943) and *The Way Ahead* (1944), where his talent for playing working-class parts in a naturalistic style shone through. The roles got bigger, and in 1945 he was given the lead as the hard-bitten criminal Leo Martin in *Appointment with Crime*. This role, however, was not the primary recommendation for the part of Dallow, Pinkie's cool henchman, because Hartnell had already played the part alongside Attenborough in the Garrick production. After *Brighton Rock*, Hartnell became somewhat typecast as a police inspector or army sergeant, playing such roles in fourteen movies in as many years, including *Carry on Sergeant* (1958). Before he finally transformed his image as Dr Who, his most popular television role had also been as a sergeant-major in *The Army Game* (1957–61). William Hartnell died in 1975 aged sixty-seven. He was a veteran of almost seventy British films.

Alan Wheatley (Fred Hale) Perhaps best known in the 1940s as the voice of BBC News for European audiences during the war, Surrey-born Alan Wheatley began a career in industrial psychology before trying his luck on the stage at twenty-one in 1927. Although he would soon go on to act with the Old Vic and appear on the New York stage, he remained a stalwart of the provincial little theatre groups, enjoying their intimacy and commitment. Wheatley's film career began modestly in 1936, but gained momentum after the war with a succession of supporting roles in films like *Jassy* and *The End of the River* (both 1947). Before *Brighton Rock*, he had appeared with Hartnell in *Appointment with Crime*. His most famous role, however, would be as the Sheriff of Nottingham in the 1950s hit television series *The Adventures of Robin Hood*. Wheatley died in 1991.

Harcourt Williams (Prewitt) The veteran Shakespearean actor Harcourt Williams was natural casting for the role of Prewitt, a faded solicitor fond of quoting from Elizabethan and Jacobean drama. Born in Croydon in 1880, Williams was touring with Ellen Terry before he was twenty, with Sir Henry Irving as one of his earliest sponsors. By the time he was fifty, he was a producer with the Old Vic Company. Laurence Olivier cast him as the French King in *Henry V* (1944), and would call on his services again for *Hamlet* (1948). Williams established himself as the definitive Prewitt in the stage play of *Brighton Rock*, and Mario Zampi must have been thinking of his performance when he was cast as a drunken old doctor in *Third Time Lucky* (1948). Williams continued to play medics, judges, lawyers and clergymen until his death in 1957.

Nigel Stock (Cubitt) The versatile actor Nigel Stock was twenty-eight when the Boultings cast him as one of Pinkie's mob, the edgy spiv Cubitt. Born in Malta, where his father was an army captain, Stock spurned a military career for a life on the stage, and appeared with Harcourt Williams at the Grafton Theatre at the age of twelve. He played two seasons at the Old Vic in his school holidays before winning a scholarship to RADA. By the late 1930s he was a regular on the London stage and had begun his film career in 'quota-quickies'. During the Second World War, he fulfilled his father's ambitions for him, attaining the rank of major in the Indian Army and serving with distinction in the Burma campaign. *Brighton Rock* was his first film after demobilisation, and followed a successful stage run in *And No Birds Sing*. The Boultings were confident enough to offer him a six-picture contract. He would go on to play supporting roles in another twenty films before his breakthrough role as the definitive Dr Watson in the *Sherlock Holmes* television series in 1964. Nigel Stock died less than two months before Hermione Baddeley in 1986.

Wylie Watson (Spicer) When the Boultings cast veteran Scottish character actor Wylie Watson as the horse-loving reluctant gangster Spicer,
they had already worked with him on their previous production *Fame
is the Spur*. He had acted in *Tawny Pipit* and *Waterloo Road* (both
1944) with George Carney, in *Temptation Harbour* (1947) with William
Hartnell, and he had co-starred with Reginald Purdell in the wartime
comedy *Pack Up Your Troubles* (1940). He had also acted for Hitchcock;
The 39 Steps (1935) and *Jamaica Inn* (1939) were among the fifty or so
films he would appear in before his last role in *The Sundowners* (1960)
at the age of seventy-one. During the filming of *Brighton Rock*, Watson
managed to fit in work on *Things Happen at Night* (1948) at Southall
studios. He died in 1966.

Charles Goldner (Colleoni) Son of a Viennese actor, Charles Goldner
was born in 1900 and began his career at the Vienna Academy of
Dramatic Art. As both an actor and producer of stage plays and opera,
he gained extensive experience all over Europe, acquiring nine languages
in the process. Fleeing Hitler's persecution of the Jews, he settled in
England. He joined the British Army in 1938, but was invalided out soon
after hostilities began, seeing out the rest of the war from London's West
End, where he produced a successful version of *The Tales of Hoffmann*.
However, it was his portrayal of the black marketeer Sugiani in the
hit play *Noose* which recommended him for the role of the crime boss
Colleoni in *Brighton Rock*. He went straight from the Boultings' film
to two more gangster roles in *No Orchids for Miss Blandish* and *Third
Time Lucky*. A connoisseur of the arts, Goldner brought a depth of
sophistication to the role of Colleoni. Greene had revised his novel after
the war to avoid accusations of anti-Semitism, emphasising Colleoni's
Italian origins, but the Boultings were not afraid to cast a Jewish actor
(with an ambition to re-create in England his continental performances
as Shylock) in the role.[48]

George Carney (Phil Corkery) By the time he took the part of the
randy bookie in *Brighton Rock*, George Carney had appeared in almost
sixty films in the previous fifteen years. He had become a mainstay of
British quota production's troupe of character actors. Many of the films
were low budget 'B's, but some – such as *In Which We Serve*, *The Stars
Look Down* (1939) and *I Know Where I'm Going* (1945) – were among
the most distinguished in the British canon. If one role was remembered,
however, it was probably as the police sergeant trying to put a stop to

George Formby's cross-dressed hi-jinks in *Come on George* (1939). The Boultings overrode Greene's rather different physical description of the Corkery character to cast Carney, whom they had already worked with on *Thunder Rock*. Tragically, he would not live to see the première of their film, dying one month before the première, shortly after his sixtieth birthday.

Reginald Purdell (Frank) The part of the blind cuckold whose laundry business provides a front for Pinkie's den of thieves was given to fifty-year-old Londoner Reginald Purdell (originally Grasdorff), a versatile actor and film-maker who had already appeared in over forty movies in seventeen years and received writing credits on a further ten. His recent acting credits included *We Dive at Dawn* (1943), *Love Story* (1944), and *Root of All Evil* (1947), while he had also contributed to the scripting of a number of generally undistinguished thrillers and comedies, among the best received of which was John Baxter's Flanagan and Allen vehicle *Dreaming* (1944). In addition, Purdell had directed two films in 1937: *Patricia Gets Her Man* and (with Arthur Woods) the Max Miller comedy *Don't Get Me Wrong*. By *Brighton Rock*, however, his career had almost run its course. He died five years later aged fifty-six.

Virginia Winter (Judy) Winter was a stage actress, specialising in revue work. Her occasional dramatic roles, however, included the part of Judy, the sluttish and adulterous wife of Frank, in the Garrick production of *Brighton Rock*. The Boultings offered her the chance to re-create the character for their film in what was her first screen role.

The Boultings had skilfully assembled a cast whose performances could bring a sense of reality to Greene's metaphysical tale of the struggle with evil in a fallen world. But, as Greene knew full well, that sense of reality could not be achieved without designers and a crew who could create a convincing *mise-en-scène*. Again, he was lucky in the Boultings' choices. The twins proved astute in engaging relatively inexperienced but highly promising creative personnel.

Production design was put in the hands of John Howell who, at thirty-three years old, was one of the more experienced members of the team. He had worked in the Gainsborough art department during the 1930s and, as a member of the RAF Film Unit, he was John Boulting's art director on *Journey Together*. The brothers employed him after the war on *Fame is the Spur* and *The Guinea Pig*. His versatility would be displayed in the contrast between the lavish set for the Cosmopolitan Hotel scenes and the decaying, claustrophobic interiors of Frank's lodging house. *Brighton Rock*'s costumes were entrusted to German-born Honoria Plesch who, when she began her association with the Boultings on *Thunder Rock*, became the youngest fully-fledged designer in the British film industry. She also designed the costumes for *Fame is the Spur*, *The Guinea Pig* and *Seven Days to Noon* (1950). To the modern viewer, Pinkie's clothes might look like 'those of the postwar spiv in all his finery' – to quote Philip Gillett – but Plesch went to great lengths to ensure that the film's original audience would be reminded of the dress of a decade before.[49] To re-create an authentic wardrobe and accessories for her gangsters, she combed the second-hand shops of the East End.

The men who were to light and photograph *Brighton Rock* were also tried and trusted members of the Boultings' team. Both in their mid-thirties, Harry Waxman and his camera operator Gilbert Taylor had worked on *Journey Together*, Waxman's first film as a director of photography. Waxman had also assisted Gunther Krampf on *Fame is the Spur*, and would again find himself working with the Boultings in the 1960s on *The Family Way* (1966) and *Twisted Nerve* (1968). His long career in British pictures would eventually peak on a Scottish headland filming *The Wicker Man* (1973). Gil Taylor, who photographed *Fame is the Spur* as well as Richard Attenborough in *School for Secrets* as camera operator, would graduate to DP on *The Guinea Pig*. He would go on to even greater glory than Waxman, becoming the leading cinematographer for Associated British during the 1950s, and working with the cream of directing talent – including Kubrick, Polanski and Hitchcock – in the 1960s and '70s. He is now best known as the director of photography on *Star Wars* (1977).

At thirty-eight, *Brighton Rock*'s production manager Gerard Bryant was the veteran of the crew, having worked in the industry for thirteen years on documentary and sponsored film production. He had been a member of the GPO and Crown film units, had directed a number of wartime shorts, and the Boultings would later employ him as their second unit director on *Seven Days to Noon*. Film editor Peter Graham Scott, on the other hand, was the baby of the bunch. With their first-choice editor, Richard Best, still battling to get *Fame is the Spur* into shape, the Boultings decided to give the precocious twenty-three-year-old Scott his first opportunity to cut a feature film, although he had already directed and edited several short documentaries, and been

second unit director on *The Shop at Sly Corner* (1946). He would go on
to direct a string of 'B' movies in the 1950s and a clutch of comedies
in the 1960s, but he would become best known as a producer and
director in television. 'Well, the Boultings would rather have someone
of twenty-three, young and keen, than some old hack,' he says, adding,
'The crew were all ex-services and they were all young.' Scott was
frustrated by the slowness of contemporary cinema: 'Films of that time
hung on shots too long. So the moment someone stopped speaking,
on the end of the word, I would cut to the next bit, which gives you
a tremendous sense of pace.'[50]

Howell's sets, Waxman's cinematography and Scott's cutting would
all play important parts in creating *Brighton Rock*'s seedy *mise-en-scène*
and drawing the audience towards Pinkie's fatal machinations; but
ultimately it would be Hans May's moody score that would bind their
contributions into an effective whole. Born Johannes Mayer in Vienna
in 1886, May had, like Goldner, crossed to Britain in the mid-1930s. As
an experienced composer, he quickly found work in the film industry.
Adept at both light and dramatic music, his most memorable scores
had been written for Gainsborough studios; notably for the melodramas
Madonna of the Seven Moons (1944) and *The Wicked Lady* (1946). The
Boultings first employed his talents on *Thunder Rock*, and he had also
scored *Fame is the Spur*. His compositions for *Brighton Rock* would
follow his dictum that film music 'must be understood by the average
audience and, at the same time, beguile the ear without being either
cheap or fantastic'.[51] He would score no further films for the Boultings,
but he would work on one more Richard Attenborough picture – *Hell
is Sold Out* (1951) – before dying in 1958.

MAKING *BRIGHTON ROCK*

Take your holidays at Brighton this year. Why? Well then you may
get your chance in films. If you don't get your chance in films, you
might get the chance to rub shoulders with some of the stars – Richard Attenborough, Bill Hartnell, Hermione Baddeley, and Carol Marsh.
Yes, they'll all be there, so don't forget to be on the look out – at
Brighton. (*Film-Shot*, vol. 2, no. 2, May 1947: 3)

One of the abiding myths of *Brighton Rock* is that it was shot almost
entirely on location at the seaside. It is a romantic notion, but, unless
one discounts the first four months of production, largely a false one.

By the contemporary standards of Italian neo-realism, *Brighton Rock* barely qualifies as a picture based on location filming.[52] However, it certainly strives for an authenticity of setting.

Early in January 1947, with Greene's screenplay adopted, 'Puffin' Asquith decided to demonstrate his loyalty to Rattigan and finally withdrew as director of *Brighton Rock*. The Boultings had doubtless anticipated this and, with *Fame is the Spur* in the can and most of the casting for *Brighton Rock* completed, confidently announced their intention to begin filming at Welwyn Studios on 17 February.[53] John Boulting would direct. That six actors – Hermione Baddeley, Richard Attenborough, William Hartnell, Harcourt Williams, Virginia Winter and Daphne Newton as the manageress of Snow's – would be re-creating their stage roles would speed rehearsals; but would also pose a problem for a director trying to develop a more subtle approach to screen acting. Attenborough remembers that the Boultings were particularly progressive in this regard and freely acknowledges the debt he owes to them in adapting his stagecraft and techniques to the demands of a cinema striving for social realism: 'It was very difficult for me to start with. My performance was a total disaster after the theatre, because I was used to having to project myself over a whole auditorium, and they had to teach me I didn't need to do that on film.'[54]

John would work with Attenborough to create psychological realism by making sure that all Pinkie's thoughts and reactions in any given situation were thoroughly thought through: 'He would then say, "Now Dick, [...] those thoughts will go through your mind *infinitely* faster than you can possibly *consciously* convey them. But they will have to *be* there and if I shoot it right, I will find those on the screen for you." He taught me that there was no such thing in cinema acting as a short cut.'[55]

Through this technique, Attenborough was able to deal with the complexities of a character that was both 'frightening' and 'absolutely fascinating': 'You had these moments of vulnerability with the ruthlessness, and even a gentleness every now and again.'[56] To further ensure Attenborough's convincing transformation into a slum kid, the twins put the well-fed Dickie on a strict diet (and even suggested he lose sleep) to try to give him that hungry and haunted look.[57]

The main headache for the Boultings, however, was not Pinkie's porkiness, but the casting of the key role of Rose. Keen to find an unknown who could be groomed for stardom, they had issued a speculative (and rather ambiguous) advertisement: 'Wanted – one sixteen or seventeen year old girl, frail, innocent, naive and tolerably but not excessively pretty. This is a tremendous opportunity for a girl with acting ability to become a star overnight. What offers?'[58]

Some 3,000 answered the call, and two or three of the most promising applicants were being auditioned daily, but a 'discovery' was proving elusive. And as the search for Rose continued, the weather took a dramatic turn for the worse. Any prospect of a February start to filming was swept away in an ice-flow of power cuts and blizzards. Towards the end of the month, a slight, brown-haired, blue-eyed girl from Rank's Company of Youth named Norma Simpson walked in from the cold and, after a screen test with Attenborough, was re-christened and anointed as Pinkie's Rose. As well as receiving an extensively documented course of instruction in waitressing, she immediately began a gruelling series of photo-shoots with Eugene Pizey on a generator-powered studio on the sound stage at Welwyn.[59] A mightily thankful John Boulting decided to use the time freed by the postponed start of filming to make a three-day good-will visit to Brighton. At a press reception at the Grand Hotel he announced that hidden cameras would be used for some of the location work to avoid attracting crowds.[60]

Principal photography eventually got underway on 6 March, almost three weeks late. The Welwyn shooting schedule was set at twelve weeks, and an arrangement negotiated with MGM to use their huge sound stage at Elstree for the larger sets needed for the hotel and dance-hall scenes. With Carl Ramon on the lookout for any inauthenticity, the unit worked first on the set representing the interior of Frank's lodging house, shooting the scenes in the hall, including the death of Spicer. Only seven actors were required before Hermione Baddeley played her first brief scene towards the end of the second week's filming. A reporter from the trade journal *The Cinema* was a regular visitor, and commented on the claustrophobic conditions which the cramped set created:

> Every member of the unit could give points to a trained contortionist after ten days shooting on the three-story composite interior of Frank's tenement house, devised by art director John Howell and built by construction manager Stan Yeomanson. Getting Harry Waxman, his camera and crew, as well as chief sound engineer Norman Coggs with his crew and equipment, in and out of Judy's room, Frank's workshop, the staircase and hall, Pinkie's room and Spicer's room has been no joke.[61]

Sound mixer Frank McNally and his team recorded a series of sounds designed to heighten the tension, including creaking floorboards, squeaking shoes and oil-less hinges.

In the third week of filming, which concentrated on the scenes in Pinkie's bedroom, the set was visited by Sir Philip Warter, chairman of ABPC, and by the Chelsea football team. The footballers were filmed for an edition of Rank's documentary series *This Modern Age* on sportsmen's lifestyles.[62] Shortly afterwards, Carol Marsh was called in to play her first scene when Rose awakes in Pinkie's bed on the morning after her wedding. Every step of Carol Marsh's preparations for her role had been given blanket coverage by the publicists at Associated British, including her arrival by coach at Welwyn studios for her first day on set. Her somewhat sanitised account of that first day (probably ghost written from interview material) appeared a few months later in *Home Review*. She recalls the messages of good wishes, including one from Attenborough, that awaited her in her dressing room and her nervousness: 'I suppose the most wonderful thing was that I, Norma Simpson, [...] with only two weeks' actual stage experience to my credit, was there at all. As an extra I would have been excited. In a dressing-room of my own with the still unfamiliar name Carol Marsh in big letters on the door, I thought perhaps I was delirious.'[63] After de-glamorising sessions in make-up and wardrobe, she was escorted on to the set by Attenborough. Technicians gave her a 'quick appraising glance' and John Boulting, 'of whom I was so much in awe', waited at the piano, gently picking out an old dance tune:

'Easy day today, Carol,' John Boulting smiled. 'You'll spend the day in bed!' We had several rehearsals of the scene first – and then before the final take he came over and talked quietly to me about the interpretation of my part, correcting the mistakes I had made, suggesting a new approach to certain lines. [...] One or two newspaper people had come down to see me do my first scene. All I actually said in the scene was 'Come in!'[64]

Fifty years on, Carol Marsh's memories were far less 'rosy', as she told the Brighton *Argus*: '[T]he Boultings were known for their sarcasm, and I was treated very badly. [...] I don't remember that much about the filming, except that I felt bullied all the time. At one time the makers even told me I had ruined their film, and if they could recast me they would. [...] It isn't a pleasant experience to look back on.'[65]

Although she admitted that much of the bullying might have been designed to extract a better performance from her, and was grateful to William Hartnell for the support he gave her, she still resented the 'pittance' of £10 per week she received under her Rank contract, and the way that she had been obliged to pay for her own accommodation in Brighton. 'At the time I was just a young girl straight out of convent school. There was no Equity protection or royalty payments, so I just went along with it, not knowing what was going on.'[66]

Some corroboration of Marsh's allegations of harsh treatment in the interests of provoking a better performance is contained in a trade journalist's report on the scene between Rose and Ida in Pinkie's bedroom, which was filmed seven weeks after Marsh first walked on set:

> To shoot this poignant scene everyone was cleared from the set except the camera crew and one camera assistant, an exponent of Chopin, who played nocturnes on the piano in a corner of the stage, right up to the moment when John Boulting called for action. But the scene didn't click. Make-up offered glycerin tears. John Boulting waved him away. He said, 'I've got to have real emotion and real tears.' Then sparing no one's feelings he tried different tactics. 'You may be from a charm school but right now I don't want charm. I want to see in front of me a little waitress who is breaking her heart ... ' Lots more of a harsh nature followed, culminating in the acid query – 'Are you really an actress – or just another publicity story?' Silence, and then Carol Marsh's tears slowly fell.[67]

By this time (ten weeks into the shooting schedule), the stress of direction was having its effect on Boulting. Production was behind schedule and he was working with a throat condition that made it difficult for him to speak. He was forced to rely heavily on 'the major', his assistant director Gerry Mitchell.

After three and a half weeks spent filming scenes at Frank's lodging house, the unit spent a further two on sequences in the Four Feathers pub. Unusually, the Four Feathers set, designed by Howell in consultation with Waxman, had a complete ceiling 11 feet high, constructed in removable sections. The set was semi-circular, showing the public, private and saloon bars, and was built in mahogany with ground glass stencilled windows. Forty extras were drafted in and real beer was served. The lightly clad extras received a 10s-a-day cold weather bonus. Additional actors joined the production, including George Carney, Basil Cunard, Alan Wheatley; and Hermione Baddeley returned after a month's break. A consummate practical joker, Baddeley marked April Fool's day by working a trick on her director. For the part of Ida, Baddeley needed her natural hair lightening. Arriving on stage with her constant companion, a brown spaniel, she was greeted by John Boulting declaring: 'Hair too dark. Would you go to hairdressing and get it fixed, please?' Half an hour later, Baddeley returned to the set leading a golden cocker spaniel that she had substituted for the original dog.[68] Before the unit moved temporarily out of Welwyn, Baddeley completed her scene with George Carney (Phil Corkery) on the set representing the gallery of the Cosmopolitan Hotel; and Attenborough and Charles Goldner filmed the meeting between Pinkie and Colleoni on the adapted set.

While a new set was constructed at Welwyn, the unit became the first to use the new state-of-the-art sound stage at MGM Elstree where a massive set, capable of accommodating 200 actors, had been built for the Cosmopolitan Hotel scenes. The set was the largest yet used for a British film and stood 45 feet high, having been constructed from the top down with a balcony suspended from the roof. It took three weeks to build and 4,000 amps to light. Initial lighting was such a gigantic operation that it took twelve hours before cameras could roll. They captured Pinkie arriving to meet Colleoni, and Pinkie and Rose's unsuccessful attempt to book a room for their honeymoon, as well as Pinkie's exit from the building and interception by a policeman on a set representing the front of the hotel.[69]

While the unit filmed at MGM, Stan Yeomanson was working hard at Welwyn to construct a replica of Brighton station, including a section of a Southern Region train. As the station bookstall was so familiar to so many holiday-makers, it was reproduced down to the last detail with 1937 books and magazines. At the end of April, the unit returned and was joined by 120 extras to film Kolley Kibber's arrival in Brighton.[70] At the last minute, John Boulting decided to include a part for Sally, the two-year-old daughter of cinematographer Harry Waxman. She played a lost girl, and the publicity department made the most of it, supplying plenty of pictures of the photo-friendly youngster.[71]

Meanwhile, the Cosmopolitan set at MGM Elstree had been replaced by a large perspective model of Brighton promenade, making full use of a double stage and showing a three-quarters-of-a-mile vista including the pier lit in pre-war style and model cars parked at the roadside. The set was built for the scene outside the Four Feathers towards the end of the film.[72] After its quick hop back to Elstree, the unit returned to a much smaller set at Welwyn where, during the ninth week of shooting it filmed a conversation between Pinkie and Rose under the pier which would be deleted from the final cut of the film.[73] A reproduction of the photo kiosk by the Palace Pier was also erected for the scene in which Rose recognises the snapshot of Spicer. Towards the end of the tenth week, filming was transferred to the basement kitchen of Frank's for the party scene; and then, in week eleven, to perspective sets of the Palace Pier. Boulting began with scenes involving Alan Wheatley as Fred, progressed to the sequence in which Pinkie threatens Rose with vitriol, and then returned to the meetings between Fred, Ida and the two girls in deck chairs.[74]

In mid-May, the set was visited by Graham Greene who viewed rushes of the previous day's filming and expressed delight in the way in which his characters had been brought to life.[75] Then, as the Boultings' thoughts began to turn to the crucial summer location filming and the need for good public relations, Richard Attenborough and Carol Marsh were dispatched to Brighton to judge a dancing contest ('Brighton Rock Challenge Cup') at Sherry's Dance Hall.[76] In the twelfth week of filming (and the last according to the Boultings' original schedule) the unit moved back to Pinkie's bedroom to shoot the emotional scene between Ida and Rose; and then on to a new set, a reproduction of a typical seaside pierrot enclosure, for Ida's song.[77] At the start of week thirteen, John Boulting interrupted filming of the pierrot sequence and took advantage of some good weather to make a day-trip to Brighton to photograph rear projection plates. These included the sequence in which an ambulance is called to take away Fred's body. Towards the end of the week, the unit moved to the set representing Brighton police station where Pinkie is issued with a warning, and Ida tries to convince the police that Rose's life is in danger.[78]

After so many weeks of bitter cold, the film unit sweated in a heat wave as June arrived. Most of the members reverted to the tropical kit they had worn in the services during the war. And the British gangster film cycle was really warming up, too, as principal photography began on *No Orchids for Miss Blandish* at Twickenham Studios. Back at Welwyn, on the Tuesday of week fourteen, the filming of *Brighton Rock* moved to a new set, Prewitt's office, where the discomfort created by the heat was worsened by the need to explode smoke puffs outside the window to simulate passing trains. Next came the register office scenes, and finally the convent scene at the close of the film.[79]

At the beginning of the fifteenth week of production, filming moved to an elaborate Howell set of the exterior of bookmaker Brewer's home constructed by master carpenter Bert Ebling on Welwyn's main sound stage. It reproduced a Brighton street complete with gas lamps and railway trains crossing a stone bridge at the rear. Scenes of the interior of Brewer's house were then filmed on another set, while John Boulting also spent a day recording dance tunes for the forthcoming dance-hall sequences. Norman Griffiths conducted a twenty-two-piece orchestra for 'More Than Ever', specially written by Leslie Julian Jones (husband of Virginia Winter). On the Wednesday and Thursday, Roy Boulting took a second unit to Brighton where production manager Gerry Bryant directed background effect and general shots of the Brighton races. Ernie Palmer was in charge of the three cameras. The unit then moved to the Palace Pier for general shots of the pier-head.[80]

Week sixteen was devoted to filming the scenes at Snow's, starting with the café itself, decorated in light green and yellow with murals of ships. Thirty extras were employed. Scenes between Pinkie and Rose in the basement of the café were then recorded on a small set. The end of the week saw the unit working on the main stage on a set representing Princes dance hall, based on the real hall at the Brighton Aquarium. Four hundred extras danced to vintage 1937 music played by Norman Griffiths and his orchestra.[81] Although Greene and Roy Boulting had originally specified a male 'crooner', John substituted the beautiful Irish actress Constance Smith, who would soon become his fiancée.[82]

It appears that, after almost four months of filming, actors and technicians were given a week's break while the final sets – the pier-head and the pier's Palace of Pleasures – were constructed. Filming resumed on the last day of June, and covered Ida and Dallow's last-minute dash through the funfair to the pier-head to save Rose, followed by the sequence at the shooting gallery. At the end of the week, the scenes of Pinkie recording his voice for Rose were shot. At the same time, Peter Graham Scott was sent to Brighton to supervise effect shots and backgrounds of tick-tack men and bookies at the race-course for the razor attack.[83] Monday to Thursday of the nineteenth week was spent filming the night scenes at the pier-head. On the Tuesday, the set was visited by the Federated Film unit who filmed the principal cast for a ten-minute feature. On 11 July, the unit vacated Welwyn, allowing International's production of the Terence Rattigan-scripted *Bond Street* to move in. The first scenes in Brighton were filmed on the Saturday night, 12 July, on the Palace Pier.[84]

As *The Cinema* reported, huge crowds gathered round the pier

8. *Filming Fred: Alan Wheatley (far left), John Boulting (centre) and his crew on Brighton's Palace Pier.*

entrance for three nights to watch the unit arrive at 10 pm for the filming, which continued until dawn:

> The first scene to be shot was at the pier-head depicting the desperate rush made by Ida Arnold, Dallow, Judy and two policemen down the pier steps on to the jetty in an attempt to avert the murder of Rose, the first part of which had been filmed in the studios. Three ex-invasion barges were used to convey the generators and sound truck to below the pier-head from Shoreham Harbour where they were loaded. [...] Arc lamps gleamed across the water and on to the pier railings until they stood out like filigree silver in the blue glare. The night scenes on the following two nights were shot at the entrance to the pier, showing the beginning of the search for Pinkie and Rose. Rain machines operated freely until a thunderstorm arrived in time for its cue at 4 a.m. and completed the job. [...] To assist lighting director Harry Waxman the full co-operation of pier and police authorities was given, so that the pier was fully lit, and neon signs and traffic lighting remained on. Night shooting finished with the tense scene between Pinkie and Rose before Pinkie is trapped and dives over the pier rails.[85]

As filming continued around the pier and seafront, Greene made another visit to the unit, this time with his mistress, the illustrator Dorothy Glover, whom he introduced as Dorothy Craigie. Unfortunately, she was recognised by one of the crew who had worked at a Paddington hotel used by the couple before the war.[86] The gossip mill, already fuelled by the burgeoning romance between John Boulting and Constance Smith, went into overdrive. Brighton, it seemed, was living up to its reputation as a hotbed of permissiveness. The tireless efforts of the publicity boys to pose Attenborough and Marsh together riding on the sun-deck of a bus or sunbathing on the beach must have created speculation about their relationship, even though Attenborough and his wife Sheila were happily together at the Grand Hotel, and Carol was walking out with the young editor Peter Graham Scott.

Filming continued in parallel with publicity and public relations activities. On 23 July, for instance, Attenborough, in costume, visited the Sussex Maternity Hospital's baby show.[87] On the following day, he was at the Princes Ballroom where nearly 500 people queued up to sign on as extras for the race-course scenes at £1.7s per day.[88]

The four-day shooting schedule at Brighton race-course over the weekend beginning 25 July was disrupted, first by poor weather and then by the chairman of the race-course lessees, Alderman S. C. Thompson, who claimed that the unit had caused damage to the turf just before the start of Brighton races. In fact, the only damage was to a patch of grass near the grandstand. The Boultings, who feared they would have to shoot the whole sequence again at another race-course at a cost of at least £10,000, issued a statement protesting against the decision.[89]

On the Monday, filming equipment was removed from the course, and on Tuesday, actors and technicians were given a further day off. While they waited for the Alderman to change his mind, Boulting filmed elsewhere in Brighton – the Lanes, the clock tower, by the Savoy and on the promenade – using a camera concealed in the back of a van to cover Fred Hale's run through the town. 'The Boultings were one of the first companies to work with hidden cameras,' Richard Attenborough has commented. 'They carried them in cardboard boxes on their shoulders [...] It was all invented for the moment. And we put them in shop windows which you couldn't see through – double glass and so on, and it was a huge advance.'[90]

On the last day of July, at a meeting of the town council, Brighton's Mayor, P. Friend-Jones, and Councilor Sherritt unsuccessfully attempted to overturn the race-course lessees' decision.[91] The Boultings responded by meeting with Brighton's Town Clerk and secretary to the lessees,

9. *Bookie's favourite: Hermione Baddeley emerges from the crush as Boulting films his race-course scenes.*

J. G. Drew, who acted as mediator in the dispute, allowing filming of general shots to recommence on 6 August at Brighton races. However, it proved impossible to take the cast back to the location and John Boulting was obliged to rely on fill-in shots on the studio lot.[92] That same evening, Boulting and members of the crew attended a farewell gala dance at the Princes Ballroom.[93] Finally, on Friday 8 August, the twins presided at an informal cocktail party at the unit's headquarters, the Grand Hotel, at which they expressed their gratitude to the town for the co-operation they had received: 'Brighton has been able to give us everything that we required for making the film, and if someone will write us a story with a Brighton setting we shall jump at the chance of coming back here again.' Guests included the Mayor, the Town Clerk, Aldermen Sherritt and Fitzgerald, the managers of the Palace Pier, Princes Ballroom and Savoy Cinema, Superintendents Crouch and Harmes, and members of the local press. Alderman Thompson pleaded a previous engagement.[94]

The unit returned to London and final post-synchronisation and editing at British National Studios, Elstree, got underway, overseen by Roy Boulting. When John retired to Constance Smith's native Ireland to nurse his health, the twins still had hopes of an October première for their film.[95] However, their *Fame is the Spur* was still awaiting release, and it was this film that premièred on 9 October, with *Brighton Rock* having to wait until the new year. Meanwhile, publicity officer Jack Worrow began to work overtime to keep the film in the news. During its production, the film had garnered 3,527 column inches of newsprint, and over 600 publicity photos had been prepared.[96]

Everything looked set fair for a film that appeared to have fulfilled the expectations created by its screenplay. Its passage to the screen, however, was not to be so smooth. With the Boultings' attention distracted by pre-production for their next feature, *The Guinea Pig*, and promotional work for *Fame is the Spur*, their most recent creation became vulnerable to the sorts of transformation for which distributors were notorious. At some point it was decided that *Brighton Rock*, as a genre crime film, was too long, and that it should run as near as possible to the standard ninety minutes, so that a second feature might be easily accommodated on the same bill. As a consequence, four or five scenes were left on the cutting-room floor. The scenes might not have been vital to narrative continuity, but they were hardly extraneous, and, in two cases, contributed significantly to the understanding of characters and to the sociological dimension of the film. The effect was to upset Greene's delicate balance between thriller and social drama in favour of the former. Consequently, the picture lost some of its moral and intellectual depth.

Next, the Boultings initially bowed to pressure from distributors Pathé to change the title of the film to *The Worst Sin*. A press book was produced with this new title, and it explains the reasoning behind the change:

> For the makers of a film based on an international best-selling novel to change the title seems, at first sight, to be a very unwise thing to do. It is like throwing away a ready-made public. But in the case of *The Worst Sin*, film version of Graham Greene's thrilling novel *Brighton Rock*, [...] change of title was inevitable. For *Brighton Rock* is well-nigh untranslatable. In the first place, the 'rock' mentioned is not the sort that rolls down cliff-faces! It is a long, hard, round stick of candy [...] popular at most British seaside resorts, but virtually unknown to the rest of the world. [...] And then, Brighton, although a famous British holiday town, is certainly not known to every foreign filmgoer.
>
> So a new name had to be found. After a high-level conference between Roy and John Boulting, makers of the film, and the foreign

department of Pathé Pictures, its distributors, *The Worst Sin* was decided upon. Like 'Brighton Rock' the new title is an extract from the script. When 'Pinkie' Brown [...] tries to persuade his teen-age Catholic wife Rose to commit suicide, she says: 'No, Pinkie. That's the worst sin of all! That's despair – there will be no forgiveness for that.'

Pathé went on to list the French, Spanish, Dutch, Swedish, Portuguese, German and Italian translations of its new title; but somehow, as far as the British title was concerned, wiser counsels prevailed at the last minute. By the second week in November, the old title had been reinstated, and on 14 November teaser ads using the words Brighton Rock began to appear in the trade press. The artwork for the advertisement announcing the film's trade show on 25 November appears to have undergone late revision, with Greene's original title pasted over Pathé's 'improvement'.[97] Unfazed, Pathé's publicists decided to capitalise on the image of a stick of rock by inserting their cockerel symbol between 'Brighton' and 'Rock', and assuring the trade that this particular 'present from Pathé' was 'stamped 100% Box-office all the way through'.

THREE
In the Can

I will draw the curtain and show the picture. Is it not well done?
(William Shakespeare, *Twelfth Night*)[1]

Hans May's cymbal roll and four doom-laden chords introduce the
leading players. A flash of lightning illuminates the brooding face
of Richard Attenborough as he glances off camera distracted by the
sound of thunder. Hermione Baddeley as Ida munches complacently
on a chocolate, while William Hartnell as Dallow reclines on his
bed and picks grimly at his fingers. As the strings gather to play a
jauntier theme, the film's title appears over a scene of frivolity on
the beach. The lettering is in the contemporary post-war fashion for
the vernacular of fairgrounds and narrow boats, but the split-screen
portraits of supporting players that follow are more in keeping with
the style of the 1930s, the film's setting.[2] Editor Peter Graham Scott
dissolves between shots of the restless ocean and the familiar pleasures
of holiday-making: picnics on the pebbles, boat trips on the Skylark,
and promenading before the Pavilion. This is the Brighton described
in the Preface that rolls over a scene of paddlers braving the Channel's
surf: 'a large, jolly, friendly seaside town in Sussex, exactly one hour's
journey from London'. The imperative to promote tourism after the
suspension of holiday-making during the war is ill-concealed.

The Preface was the Boultings' concession to anxious town coun-
cillors who were concerned that the image of their resort, already
tarnished by Greene's novel, might suffer further at the hands of film-
makers. Fearing opposition to location shooting, the twins had agreed to
a disclaimer stressing the historical nature of the roguery depicted. The
Boultings thought that, 'in the circumstances', the concession was 'a fair
one to make'. However, the Preface's reference to 'another Brighton
of dark alleyways and festering slums' from which 'the poison of crime

and violence and gang warfare began to spread' probably served only to kindle memories of 'trunk' murders and race-course gangs. The credit for banishing 'that other Brighton' is given to the local police. The irony of this attribution will be made clear in the final chapter of this book but, in the opening of *Brighton Rock*, it remains unrevealed behind the cheery bustle of May's score and breezy certainty that the other Brighton is 'now happily no more'.

The relaxed atmosphere is maintained with a pan along the body of one of the holiday-makers asleep in the sun, his face covered by a newspaper. Its story of the discovery of a man's body echoes our own discovery of the newspaper's owner, stretched out on the pebbles.[3] As we read the details of the case, the film's mood begins to darken.

Evening Argus, Tuesday 11th June 1935
BRIGHTON GANGSTER'S BODY FOUND
Gravel Pit Discovery
by Peter Black

The mutilated body of William Kite, aged 45, leader of a local race gang, was found this morning in a disused gravel pit. Police believe his death to be the result of gang warfare which followed an exposé of the Slot-machine Racket in the 'Daily Messenger'. A rival gang is said to suspect Kite of revealing certain facts to Fred Hale, a former *Evening Argus* crime reporter. Chief Insp. Oswald Bryant, who is in charge of the investigation, went immediately to the scene accompanied by Det. Sgt Kitchener.

We are reading a mock-up of the genuine evening paper of the Brighton area, and the by-line of the story belongs to the man who was actually one of its reporters at the time of filming. Greene's novel makes it clear that the 'rival gang' is 'Colleoni's mob' and that Kite was murdered at a London railway station before his body was dumped. The murder is actually described by his killer, Raven, in Greene's 1936 novel *A Gun for Sale*, but the body is left at a bookstall rather than a gravel pit.[4] This discrepancy is probably a function of a last-minute decision to drop the opening scene of the shooting script and instead to use the newspaper device to supply a back-story to the action of the film.[5]

ALTERNATIVE OPENINGS

Following his Bank Holiday custom, Lobby will be at Brighton today. Study his picture above and when you spot him show him your copy of today's *News Chronicle* and say 'You are Mr. Lobby Lud. I claim the *News Chronicle* prize.' (*News Chronicle*, 3 August 1936)

The third draft of *Brighton Rock*'s shooting script, preserved in the Terence Rattigan collection of the British Library, begins with a sequence in Frank's lodging house, the headquarters of Pinkie's gang. Frank's wife, Judy, is in their bedroom. With her foot 'encased in a mule with a broken heel' she pushes a glass and what is left of a half bottle of gin under the bed – 'her idea of clearing up'. She crosses the hall to Frank's workroom where her blind husband is pressing a suit in a cloud of steam. She lights a cigarette for him and he tells her that she is a good wife. In response, 'Judy looks at him coldly and with a suggestion of distaste'. When Dallow, 'a large, muscular man with an expression of brutal simplicity' enters and inquires about breakfast, it becomes evident from their 'casual embrace' that he and Judy are conducting an affair under Frank's nose (and in front of his sightless eyes). Dallow wants to know the whereabouts of the rest of the gang. Cubitt has gone out to buy a newspaper, Spicer is making breakfast and Pinkie remains in his room. Nobody, it seems, is prepared to disturb his mourning for Kite. As the sequence moves into the basement kitchen,

10. Steamy stuff: Reginald Purdell, Virginia Winter and William Hartnell in the deleted opening scene.

the transition aided by the clouds of steam from Frank's iron, the full squalor of the living arrangements (physical and moral) is presented. Amid the dirty linen and piles of unwashed dishes, Spicer eats sardines from the tin and Judy comments on the state of her marriage: 'He don't see and I don't care.' The main topic of conversation, however, is Pinkie. He has been moping in his room for nearly a week, behaviour which Spicer regards as 'morbid'. The exchange between Dallow and Judy that follows is important in establishing Pinkie's character and his relationship with his dead mentor:

> DALLOW: He's only a kid an' he worshipped Kite.
> JUDY: He's got odd tastes.
> DALLOW: Kite found Pinkie playing in the garbage down Nelson Place and he made a man of him.
> JUDY: Did he? Wouldn't have known it.

Kite's sexuality is established in neither the novel nor the film, but Judy's comments come close to implying a paedophilic relationship with Pinkie, which, in turn, might help to explain Pinkie's disturbed personality.[6] But however we interpret the references to 'odd tastes' and making 'a man of him', Dallow here gives the only clues to Pinkie's origins. With the deletion of the scene went any reference to the slum childhood that assumes such a prominence in the novel.[7] Gone, too, were Spicer's comments on the conventions and expectations of gang conflict in the period: 'Anyone who leads a mob's liable to be carved one day. They didn't mean to kill Kite.' These comments were also useful in establishing Pinkie's difference and the inappropriateness of his responses, even within the underworld community. Spicer's discourse is curtailed by the return of Cubitt with the *Daily Messenger*, the point at which the scene in the final cut of the film begins.

That the sequence was filmed is evident from production photographs preserved in the collection of Canal + Image UK.[8] Peter Graham Scott believes the scene was intact when it left his cutting room. Its loss is a significant one in establishing characters, relationships and motivations. *Brighton Rock* would now benefit from its restoration.

In the shooting script, Fred Hale's arrival in Brighton follows Cubitt's discovery of the Kolley Kibber schedule in the *Daily Messenger*. In the final cut, however, the station scene has been brought forward, perhaps to prevent confusion that might result from a direct transition between the newspaper that covers the man's face on the beach and the one that Cubitt brings into Frank's.[9] Instead, the close-up of the newspaper on the beach is juxtaposed with a mobile news hoarding announcing Kolley Kibber's presence in town. Its trolley trundles past Kolley as he disembarks from the train and pauses apprehensively to light his pipe before depositing his card at the bookstall. Much of the original scene was consigned to the cutting-room floor. Molly and Delia, the two girls that Fred later meets on the pier, were to have made their first appearance trying to claim the *Daily Messenger* prize but accosting the wrong man.[10] Also deleted was the sequence in which a family of holiday-makers, much like the one in Carol Reed's Brighton-set *Bank Holiday* (1938), discover the card Fred leaves at the bookstall. In fact, much time and effort was lavished on the creation of the station scene to very little effect. Stan Yeomanson's elaborate mock-up of the station and train are only glimpsed, and the 120 extras employed on the scene appear an extravagance. In fact, the shot of the crowd at the ticket barrier looks suspiciously like second unit footage of the real station. Unfortunately, too, the 'lost girl' played by Harry Waxman's daughter Sally remains part of *Brighton Rock*'s lost footage.

THE HUNTING OF HALE

> ... for now the thought
> Both of lost happiness and lasting pain
> Torments him; round he throws his baleful eyes,
> That witnessed huge affliction and dismay
> Mixed with obdúrate pride and steadfast hate.
>
> (John Milton, *Paradise Lost*, 1: 54–8)

An atmospheric establishing shot of the north end of Brighton's Regency Square dissolves into Cubitt's arrival in Frank's kitchen. Nigel Stock as Cubitt looks every inch the spiv – Clark Gable moustache, loud tie and trilby at a rakish angle – and the kitchen is perfectly realised. Its decaying plaster reveals the brickwork beneath and its barred basement windows suggest the entrapment of the characters. This is our first view of the fallen world inhabited by Brighton's lost souls. The short sequence in which Pinkie's gang learn about Fred's masquerade as Kolley and debate the wisdom of telling their leader sketches out the characters of Dallow, Spicer and Cubitt. Dallow is a light-footed man of action, prepared to make decisions and take the consequences. Spicer is old, cowardly, slow on the up-take and prepared to give people the benefit of the doubt. Cubitt is a chancer who lives on his wits, as

Stock indicates with his habit of idly tossing coins. He is not as afraid as Spicer is of Pinkie. Kite's gang encompasses the three narcissistic criminal types that Andrew Spicer suggests are typically portrayed in British films of this period: the spiv (Cubitt), the gangster (Dallow) and the delinquent (Pinkie).[11] But, while the mob begins to take shape, the loss of the earlier footage at Frank's means that Judy's presence at the breakfast table is unexplained and Frank is yet to be seen.[12]

The first shots of Attenborough as Pinkie brilliantly convey the menace and psychopathology of the boy gangster. They follow the shooting script to the letter:

> (set up) 18 MLS Interior Pinkie's bedroom
> We don't see his face, but we see his hands playing endlessly at a piece of string, tying knots. CAMERA finishes on a CLOSE SHOT of Pinkie's hands and the newspaper photograph.
> 19 LCU Pinkie's face
> His dead eyes are fixed on the photograph of Fred

As the first glimpse of a villain this would be bettered only by the shaft of light that strikes Harry Lime in *The Third Man* (1949). For the Catholic Pinkie, the string is a perversion of the rosary, and he twists it like a ligature, ironically bringing his hands together in the symbol of prayer as he does so. The action speaks eloquently of violence and obsession, and the credit must go to Attenborough who introduced the cat's cradle motif into his stage performance at the Garrick.[13] When Boulting finally offers the close-up of Pinkie's face against the case-less pillow, our worst fears are confirmed. The face, with its cod eyes and tight lips, is at once brutal and angelic: the face of a sadistic choir boy. No words are necessary.

More hospitable hands than Pinkie's serve Fred a drink as the action dissolves to the Four Feathers pub.[14] It is an immaculate piece of set design, as authentic as the real beer that was served to the actors. Anonymous in Greene's novel, the pub was given the name 'The Feathers' in Rattigan's film treatment. Greene seems to have added the 'Four', thus evoking the famous imperialist epic produced by his original sponsor in movieland, Alexander Korda (*The Four Feathers*, Zoltan Korda, 1939). The name also connotes the cowardice that is gripping Fred as he downs his gin and spots Pinkie's reflection in the mirror – another product of Rattigan's treatment. In casting Alan Wheatley as Fred, the Boultings again demonstrate flawless judgement.

11. *Razors and laces: Fred (Alan Wheatley) with the blind hawker.*

Wheatley knows just how to play the nervous, shabby journalist. He clings to the bar, his eyes searching for a bolthole like a rodent cornered by a predator. In contrast, Pinkie's eyes stare distractedly away as he becomes increasingly irritated by the singing of Ida in the adjacent bar. As Dallow and Cubitt reject Fred's desperate bribes and issue their intimations of his imminent mortality, Pinkie's nerves finally snap and he turns suddenly, demanding that someone shuts 'that brass's mouth' and sweeping the glasses from the bar in a demonstration of temper. The cash register rings up 'No Sale', as if to mock Fred's attempts to buy off his persecutors. The barman who voices his objection is Carl Ramon, the former member of the Sabini gang who acted as an adviser on the production.

The threat of the razor is ever-present in the scene. The impetuous Cubitt is itching to pull his 'chiv' from his pocket and 'lace' Fred, but the more cautious Pinkie stills his hand. When the gangsters leave the pub, Fred's instinct is to flee, but he is reminded of what fate might await him outside when he finds the door blocked by a half-blind hawker of razors and laces. Instead, he scuttles to the public bar, where Ida is holding court. He tries to pick her up, but she is loyal to her courtiers, the Trudy brothers. This fraternal pairing is not mentioned in Greene's novel, and seems to be an oblique self-reference to the brace of brothers responsible for the film – T[he] rudey brothers, perhaps. The two actors remain unidentified.

It is ironic that what is probably the most celebrated sequence of location filming in British cinema begins on the floor at Welwyn Studios. Fred steps out of the Four Feathers on to an exterior set dressed with a lamp-post and telephone box. The spiv in the camel coat (a walk-on part for Ronald Shiner, who would become one of Britain's most successful comedy actors) announces his membership of a race-course gang by sending a tick-tack message to a colleague across the street at the phone box. Boulting attempts to disguise the brevity of the signalling distance, together with the gap between the two halves of his set, with an ingenious whip pan. As Fred makes his escape in the direction of the Lanes, the location sequence gets underway. The sequence has no counterpart in Greene's novel and was created purely for its cinematic qualities, its role in building suspense, and its potential to locate the action of the film in a recognisable place. It succeeds wonderfully, covering Alan Wheatley's movements naturalistically with concealed and mobile cameras, and using the authentic geography of Brighton. Indefatigable *Brighton Rock* researcher Maire McQueeney has traced Fred's progress through the mean streets of Brighton: from Market Square, to Meeting House Lane, Union Street, North Street, the clock tower, Queens Road to the station where a second whip pan reveals the presence of Cubitt and his friend the tick-tack man. Turning back, Fred hops on a convenient bus back down Queens Road (although in 1937 it would have been one of the trams described in the first paragraph of Greene's novel).[15] Quickly alighting, he is off into North Street. As he runs down Church Street, nearly colliding with two cyclists, we can see Carlton Hill in the distance. Pre-war, this was the site of Nelson Place, and the breeding ground of Pinkie's delinquency. But Fred turns off at Marlborough Place and charges past the Royal Pavilion towards the Palace Pier.[16] Ever the pessimist, he carries his raincoat, expecting bad weather. All the time, the man in pursuit keeps one hand on the chiv in his pocket. The man on the run is a recurrent motif in the films of the early post-war years. It refers to the dislocation and displacement, as well as the genuine feelings of persecution, that were so much a part of the times. Fred, footloose and peripatetic, contrasts with Pinkie, an adamantine fixture on his home turf.

The sequence is cut to Hans May's tense score, but it was originally intended that it should be accompanied by Fred's voiceover. The script for this might have been written by Samuel Beckett:

'Got to get out of Brighton and not come back. Get out of Brighton. 12.10 train. In town before they close. Go into the office and say "Get another Kolley Kibber, I'm through." On the streets. Who cares. I'm alive, aren't I? I'm alive. I've got a right to be alive. That boy's crazy. Get out of Brighton 12.10 train. In town before they close. A man got a right to live. Bad for my heart. Doctor said I'd got to go easy. They've got no right to scare me. Get out of Brighton. Go to the police, say "I got to live"...' At this point he is confronted by Cubitt and tick-tack man at the Station. 'They daren't touch me in the open. Keep in the open, they daren't touch me in the daylight. They'd have got on the train with me, waited till the tunnel, keep away from the Station, can't touch me in the open, if I wasn't alone, if I wasn't alone. I'll pick up a girl, that's what I'll do, pick up a girl, that's easy, anybody can pick up a girl, pick up a girl, nobody can touch me if I'm not alone.'

The voiceover would have been useful in signalling Fred's heart condition (the cause of his death according to the post mortem) which otherwise is only subtly alluded to when his hand goes to his heart outside the Four Feathers. However, to give Fred a voiceover would have privileged his viewpoint over that of other characters, and it would not be surprising if it was dropped on that ground. Fred is not the protagonist of *Brighton Rock*, and he will quickly disappear from the narrative, just as the woman on the run, Janet Leigh's character, disappears from *Psycho* (Alfred Hitchcock, 1960).

At the end of his run, Fred bustles through the turnstiles of the Palace Pier and makes his way up the crowded boards, past promenaders and sunbathers. Spotting a free deck chair, he flops down beside the two girls who, in the deleted scene at the station, had accosted the wrong Kolley Kibber.[17] The transition from location to Welwyn set is seamless and a tribute to the meticulous detail of the film's production design and Harry Waxman's expert lighting. Ironically, Molly and Delia are waiting for the arrival of Kolley, their *Daily Messenger*s at the ready, but they still fail to recognise him. Fred, who needs to be 'a fast worker', tries inexpertly to pick up both girls, undeterred by their collusive whispers and 'hideous cackles', as the shooting script describes them. Joan Sterndale-Bennett as the 'pale, bloodless' Delia and Lina Barrie as the 'fat and spotty' Molly do not quite match their script descriptions, but both supply delightful and believable cameos.[18] Molly's cackle is turned into a nervous laugh by the sudden appearance of Pinkie and the boys, urging Fred to 'come for a walk' with them. Wheatley soundlessly conveys the reaction Greene describes in his book: 'The ground moved under his feet, and only the thought of where they might take him while he was unconscious saved him from fainting. But even then common pride, the instinct not to make a scene, remained overpoweringly strong; embarrassment had more force than terror.'[19] Gil Taylor's camera uses the sides of Pinkie and Dallow to frame the panicking Fred. Attenborough makes the most of the shot by maintaining an irritated twitch of the finger on the left of the screen. The tension mounts again as Fred bolts, leaving a collapsed chair and Cubitt, who bids a polite farewell to the ladies with a doff of his trilby.

Ida is a potential saviour but Fred is almost too preoccupied to appreciate his good fortune in running into her. She greets him with a laugh more piercing even than Molly's and thus continues the chorus of mocking laughter that follows Fred to his end. Ida senses an opportunity to make some easy money and drops a heavy hint that she is short of cash. The note she receives from Fred is the product of 'a good day at Leicester (races)'. This is the first of the references to Leicester – Attenborough's home town – that replace the Nottingham references of the novel. This one also leads to Fred's racing tip: Black Boy, a veiled allusion to Pinkie's character.[20] The most significant moment in the scene, however, is Ida's comment that she is 'a stickler where right is concerned'. 'Right' will be her motivation in bringing Fred's killer to justice. Baddeley plays Ida with the maternal carnality that Greene's text seemed to call for, but the author was never happy with her casting. He had been scathing about her performance in the stage adaptation of his novel: 'Her grotesqueness is all wrong for the part [...] She shouts all the time and has no variety in her voice [...] she is meant to be a natural amateur bawd not an oddity whom nobody could possibly sleep with.'[21] His problem seems to have been that Baddeley was simply not sexy enough to embody the kind of eroticised mother figure he had in mind.[22] For Greene, she lacked the subtle and dangerous contradictions of his creation.

FRED'S DEATH RIDE

... Hail, horrors, hail,
Infernal world, and thou, profoundest Hell,
Receive thy new possessor ...
(Satan in Milton's *Paradise Lost*, 1: 250–2)

In Greene's book, the details of Hale's murder remain obscure. The conclusion of most interpreters is that the unfortunate Kolley was abducted to a kiosk below the promenade and killed by having a stick of Brighton rock forced into his throat. His body was then disposed of in the sea. The water dissolved the offending confectionery and allowed the coroner to reach a verdict of death by natural causes.[23] The choice of such a bizarre method of murder directs us to its symbolic significance. The boy gangster has used a child's comforter as a deadly expression of his rage. He has expressed his latent homosexuality by using a pink phallic object in a grim parody of fellatio. As a boy who considers himself 'real Brighton', the rock is his personal symbol. It stands for his condition: his inability to escape his state of sin.

In the film adaptation, things are different. Greene's screenplay, like Rattigan's treatment before it, is happy to accept the idea of the pier as a terminal zone, which was first developed in Frank Harvey's stage play. The Dante's Inferno ride – '90 seconds of pure 'orror' – becomes Hale's rollercoaster to Hades.[24] However, in Rattigan's version, Fred completes a circuit with Ida before his solo spin and it is Dallow and Cubitt who are his executioners while Ida retrieves her hankie. Greene's script, more appropriately, makes Pinkie the killer, and John Boulting added the fairground barker tempting the unfortunate Hale to his doom. Boulting was probably also responsible for the late addition of the blind man and his granddaughter, the only witnesses to Fred's fatal fall, although blind men are a recurring motif in Greene's novel. They stand for the metaphorical blind eye that is turned by public and police towards Brighton's *demi-monde*, or for the spiritual blindness within the fallen world that is Pinkie's environment.

The Dante's Inferno ride is an example of what Peter Wollen has termed the 'vernacular fantastic', a glimpse of the cheap-but-exotic constructs of popular entertainment that is typical of the spiv film cycle.[25] The ride provides a deliciously macabre climax to the film's first act. Waxman's expressionist cinematography combines spooky close-ups with dizzying point-of-view shots of demonic apparitions as the train rattles round its circuit above the rushing waters accompanied by the screams of the damned.[26] The sequence cleverly evokes the hellfire and torments that so obsess the boy gangster, and supplies a genuinely cinematic solution to the problem posed by the invisibility of Hale's murder in Greene's book. In fact, it is a solution so in keeping with the spirit and architecture of 'Greeneland' that it is a wonder that the author failed to find it in the first place. The dark tunnel of torments is the perfect killing ground for Pinkie, haunted as he is by fears, not only of the afterlife, but of sexual penetration. The erotic symbolism of the tunnel is heightened by the young swain who first sits next to Fred and tries to entice his girl to join him on the ride. When Pinkie, the virgin killer and killer virgin, replaces the frustrated swain, he adds teeth to the tunnel, transforming it into a *vagina dentata*. His need for revenge satisfied, Pinkie crosses quickly to the Palace of Pleasure's shooting gallery where he endeavours to set up a 'phony alibi' with the hostile stallholder, Bill (Wally Patch). 'The shelves of dolls stared down', Greene tells us, 'with a glassy innocence, like Virgins in a church repository.' As befits a dead-eyed killer, Pinkie's aim is faultless and, rejecting a prize of chocolates or cigarettes, he opts for the doll with the 'yellow hair'. The doll reminds him of 'church' and its acquisition prefigures his possession of Rose. The brief scene serves to emphasise Pinkie's sociopathic nature – his apparent lack of concern or remorse in sending a man to his death – and his complete lack of conventional consumer vices. A teetotaller who neither smokes nor craves confectionery (he prefers it as a weapon), it seems his body is a temple. His mind, of course, is somewhere else entirely.

THE ALIBI

To do aught good never will be our task,
But ever to do ill our sole delight …
(Satan addressing the fallen angels in Milton's *Paradise Lost*,
1: 159–60)

In Greene's novel and Rattigan's film treatment, Pinkie gives the doll he has won to a waitress at the pier tea room in a further attempt to establish his alibi. His gang then joins him for a fish and chips lunch. The screenplay relocates the lunch to Frank's and retains the doll, not only for the sake of continuity editing, but because the sight of Attenborough tugging out its hair is an eloquent image of innocence violated. It tells us just what we need to know about Pinkie's cruelty and misogyny. In its association with the Virgin Mary, the doll stands for the mortal sin Pinkie has committed in defiance of his church, but it also provides a link to that other virgin whom the boy will meet in the next scene. Prophetically, the meeting between Pinkie and Rose is presaged by the breaking of the doll as it rolls off Pinkie's bed.

The scene in the boy's bedroom also underlines the differences between Pinkie and the rest of the gang who lodge at Frank's.[27] While

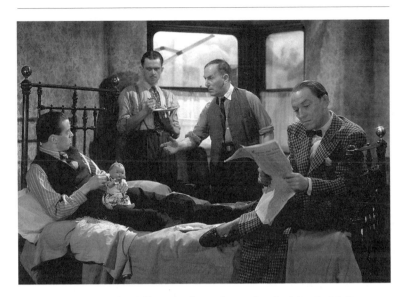

12. *Four men and a doll: Richard Attenborough, Nigel Stock, Wylie Watson and William Hartnell.*

they live largely for the present, Pinkie prides himself on his vision and his ability to anticipate danger. He is the grand strategist of the group, contemptuous of the cowardice and complacency of the others. 'Sometimes,' he complains, 'I get tired of working with a mob like you', and pines a little for his lost father figure, Kite. When the others shy away from retrieving the Kolley Kibber card from Snow's restaurant, Pinkie decides to do the job himself. As he leaves to confront the danger created by Spicer's incompetence, he pulls on his jacket and we see the pleats running down the back in long stripes like the cuts of a razor.

While the pier with its sideshows and shooting galleries is Pinkie's domain, Snow's is not. Its name reflects the whiteness of its tablecloths.[28] It has pretensions to gentility, which alienate the boy from Paradise Piece. As he sits uneasily at the table with the yellow flowers, we feel the disapproval of the uniformed waitresses who chatter and preen in the background. His awkwardness is given physical form as he noisily upsets the pepper pot. Knowing this is not a place for boys like him, and driven by the resentment this knowledge provokes, Pinkie asserts his pride by demanding service. The strict protocols of genteel eating are invoked to deny the legitimacy of his claim to the table of his choice. His misogyny and sense of inferiority rise in him like bile as he experiences the icy welcome of the supercilious waitress, played by that most prolific of character actresses Marianne Stone.[29]

He is quickly assigned a waitress suited to his status, the inexperienced Rose. For Rose, 'a pale, thin, washed-out child' (script), Snow's is the opportunity to better herself. The bitter irony, of course, is that instead of meeting a rich and cultured customer who might take her far away from her origins, she meets Pinkie, a doomed boy from her own slum neighbourhood. Her first words to Pinkie as she catches him feeling under the tablecloth – 'Have you lost something, sir?' – seem prosaic enough until we realise that Pinkie has indeed lost something that perhaps only Rose can help him to recapture: his state of grace. His immortal soul has lost its way to heaven, and the love of Rose might redirect it, but Pinkie sees only the threat she poses to his safety in this world. His insecurity is intensified by the arrival outside of an ambulance to pick up the body of his victim. It spurs him to curb his usual hostility and attempt to turn on the charm. He forces a smile, but, as Greene reminds us, 'he couldn't use those muscles with any naturalness'.[30] He tries flattery and an attempt to construct a bond between them: 'I like a girl who's friendly. Some of these here, blimey, they freeze you [...] You're sensitive, like me.' Rose, eager to please and fearful of giving offence, basks in his attentiosn and accepts his offer of a date with alacrity. As Pinkie leaves he gives her a last chance to avoid involvement, but she tells him proudly that she never forgets a face, and Pinkie smiles in the knowledge that another victim has presented herself.

THE DEAD MAN SPEAKS

> She believed in ghosts, but you couldn't call that thin transparent exist-
> ence life eternal. (*Brighton Rock*, p. 36)

As the action returns to the Four Feathers, the trope of the newspaper headline is used again to inform us that Ida has been giving evidence at the inquest on Kolley Kibber. When Jim the publican (Basil Cunard) folds his *Evening Gazette*, Ida is revealed in her pierrot costume. In the novel and play, Ida is a barmaid; but for the film, Greene makes her a seasonal entertainer. This is a clever ploy that emphasises both her in- and out-of-placeness. It is strange to see a pierrot in a pub, but not at the seaside. She is, at the same time, a visitor and one of the town's work force; and her status as a migrant worker signifies the temporary and liminal nature of so much that takes place at holiday resorts. Ida mediates uneasily between the contra-visions of Brighton as Utopia and dystopia. Greene may have remembered a particular Brighton pierrot recalled by Leonard Goldman in his memoirs: 'One of the [pierrot] companies I particularly remember was Ouida MacDermott and her troupe. The comedian referred to her as: Oh, you Ida MacDermott! She was a singer of some ability and her rendering of the sentimental *I'm a Dreamer* has lingered in my mind.'[31]

Ida is quickly joined by Phil Corkery, 'broad, hearty, full of vitality' (shooting script), who does not appear to share her scepticism about the inquest verdict. Challenging Phil's assertion that 'the dead can't speak', Ida sets out to demonstrate her psychic powers by selecting random letters from the newspaper. In Greene's novel and Rattigan's film treatment, Ida's seance takes place in London, in her rooms near Russell Square. She uses a ouija board rather than a newspaper and her companion in Spiritualism is an elderly neighbour named Old Crowe.[32] The spirits encourage Ida to seek the assistance of Phil Corkery who, in a neat telescoping of the narrative, replaces Old Crowe in the final film version.

Michael Sheldon has suggested that the three words spelled out by Ida's board in the novel – SUKILL, FRESUICILLEYE, PHIL – may constitute clues to the solution of the first Brighton trunk murder for which Greene may have had privileged information through either extra-sensory perception or direct involvement.[33] For the film, Greene rearranges the letters of the principal spirit message to read EYESUICILLFRE, and has the publican write them out in chalk like the odds on a bookmaker's slate. For Ida the letters are a clear indication that 'Someone drove him [Fred] to suicide', but there is a suggestion that Ida's is, at best, a partial interpretation of the spirit message. There remain two 'Ls' which she cannot fit into her interpretive schema. In keeping with his general contempt for what her character represents, Greene seems to be saying that she cannot recognise the truth when it is chalked up in capital letters in front of her.

GOING COURTING

What was most evil in him needed her: it couldn't get along without goodness. [...] She was good, he'd discovered that, and he was damned: they were made for each other. (*Brighton Rock*, p. 126)

Boulting dissolves from the resolute Ida to the inky waters beneath the

Palace Pier. Above, Pinkie is as we see him in the film's opening credits: leaning over the railings, lit from below by reflections from the water. Rose runs to him across the set built in perspective on the sound stage at Welwyn. As they face us at the rail, the arches of the concert hall stretching out behind them like the nave of a church, they might almost be standing at the altar. The *mise-en-scène* is Gothic and melodramatic. As flashes of lightning illuminate the scene, the pier's loudspeakers are broadcasting Mendelssohn's evocation of stormy weather at sea. Rose is desperate to please her new boyfriend, but blithely continues to maintain that the man who left the card at Snow's was not Fred. Pinkie determines that a warning is in order and draws her into a shelter as, symbolically, the rain begins to fall on them.

The pier end is Pinkie's *sanctum maleficarum*. It is his site of contemplation and torments, the place where (according to the novel) he met Kite, murdered Fred and now meets Rose for his own inverted form of courtship. His intention is to ensure Rose's silence by seducing her into a devotion that he will inevitably betray. The pain she will know will be the pain he has suffered throughout his adolescence: a love lost, a fall from grace. Her humiliation will be his revenge on the Virgin, like the pulling out of the doll's golden hair. To ensure her seduction, it might be advisable to conceal his sadistic impulses, but Pinkie is compelled to express them; a sign of his troubled and maladjusted masculinity. Instead of a tender kiss he threatens her with acid. Intimidation is, after all, his profession. And Rose, whom we might expect to take flight, instead is drawn by the magnetism of his evil. Something within her is kindled by his capacity for misanthropy. She appears to be in a state of rapture, an instrument of some greater will, a missionary sent to offer him salvation.

The sequence in which Pinkie threatens Rose in the shelter is artfully lit by Waxman, who keeps Attenborough largely in shadow while bathing Carol Marsh's face in mellow light. Marsh effectively suggests the awe in which Rose holds Pinkie by staring wistfully into the distance and meeting his gaze only when forced. As she basks in quasi-religious devotion to the idea of romantic love, the camera pans down to the hand that rests on what we assume is a bottle of vitriol in Pinkie's pocket.[34] His vitriol, like his razor, is a fetish object to which his libido has been transferred. His hand narcissistically returns to the weapon in his pocket in a signature auto-erotic gesture. He refers to a girl's face being 'splashed' because she 'got mixed up with a mob', and the threat he is imparting is clear enough, but the shooting script indicates that something more explicit was planned before the intervention of the censor:

(Set-up) 137   C.U. ROSE
PINKIE: Rose, you ever read about Peggy Brown?
             C.U. of hand on the vitriol bottle
ROSE: What happened to her?
138   C.U. PINKIE
PINKIE: She lost her eyes. They splashed vitriol in her face.
139   C.U. ROSE (lightning)
ROSE: What's vitriol?
140   C.U. of hand in pocket – PINKIE takes out the bottle and
             spills a little on the Pier planks.
141   C.U. Pier planks. The acid hisses like steam.
142   C.U. ROSE and PINKIE
ROSE: Pinkie, you wouldn't.
PINKIE: I was pulling your leg. This is just spirit.

The intended sequence is very close to the original text, and Greene must have been sorry to lose the perverse pun linking the disfiguring acid with the Holy Ghost. However, he manages to retain the association of Pinkie with Satan via his 666 telephone number, even though he is obliged to add a five to the three sixes.

Considering the amount of money and effort that went into its creation – an elaborate replica hall and 400 extras – the scene at Sherry's dance hall (or 'Harry's' as it appears in the script) is disappointing. A production still showing Rose and Pinkie in long shot with the dancers and orchestra indicates the scale of the enterprise.[35] The only footage to survive the final cut, however, was a complex crane shot which tracks across the musicians to the figure of nineteen-year-old Constance Smith gently warbling 'More Than Ever', the song written for the production by Leslie Julian Jones. The camera then cranes down over the heads of the dancers towards Rose and Pinkie seated at a table. For Greene, the *palais de dance* is a secular church where a crooner replaces the priest, singing of 'love of a kind, music of a kind, truth of a kind' to a crowd that is 'reverent, absorbed' (shooting script). The ceremony performed by the musicians and dancers is, however, an anaemic affair compared to the sanguineous communion of Rose and her own ersatz priest, Pinkie. He too speaks of love and truth above the music he describes as 'real'. Rose is enchanted by the ballroom, but Pinkie remains tormented with disgust at the sight of the 'two-backed beasts' shuffling in waltztime.[36]

The scene is important first in establishing the ages of Pinkie and Rose. The congruency of their ages is in stark contrast to the gulf in their respective experiences of the world.[37] While Rose's 'wide unfledged eyes' signify her innocence, Pinkie's dark probing gaze communicates his anger and a sense of disillusionment that belies his years.[38] Second, while the scene reveals their shared belief in Roman Catholicism it also suggests that, spiritually, there is a chasm between them. Rose is 'soft', pure as the white ice cream she spoons from the silver chalice. She believes in 'heaven' and imagines she has experienced 'love'. Pinkie, on the other hand, has seen enough of 'love' to hold it in contempt. For him, love is not an emotion but an act performed before a reluctant spectator. He picks up her fallen rosary (her name proclaims its appropriateness to her faith) like a man rediscovering something he lost in his youth, something once familiar. As he asserts the existence of hell and its torments, the camera inches towards a tighter close-up and we begin to appreciate the earthly torments he is already suffering.

While the cinematography does not quite do justice to the setting, the sentiments expressed are powerful. They would have been more powerful without the respect shown to the sensitivities of the censor. When Pinkie declares his contempt for love in the shooting script he alludes specifically to its physical aspects: 'You don't know what it's all about. Saturday nights. I've watched it. I know love.' Boulting judiciously drops the reference to 'Saturday nights'. At the behest of the censor, he also cuts Pinkie's soft intonement of a fragment of the Catholic Mass – '*Agnus Dei qui tollis peccata mundi*' (Lamb of God who taketh away the sins of the world) – on the grounds that it is a blasphemy from his lips.[39] It is a significant loss because, in the Mass, the words are a prelude to a request for the forgiveness of sin, and show that Pinkie has not totally abandoned hope of salvation.

TAKING CARE OF BUSINESS

I have often been of service to the 'boys' – it pays a professional racegoer to be, and politeness costs nothing. I have never refused to subscribe a 'quid' or so to every subscription list that has been placed before me by 'responsible' people. (T. H. Day, *Leaves from a Bookmaker's Book*, 1930)[40]

In the two scenes that follow, Pinkie's intimidation of Rose is mirrored in the way he deals with the rebellious bookmaker Brewer. On returning

13. *Lacing Brewer: Hartnell, Attenborough and Harry Ross.*

to Frank's he overhears Spicer expressing doubts about his leadership and the wisdom of challenging Colleoni, the most powerful of the local gangsters and the man responsible for Kite's death. This stirs Pinkie's pride and anger and fuels his paranoia. His suspicion that Spicer is not to be trusted is confirmed, and an intimation of Spicer's eventual fate is given, when Pinkie tenderly caresses the broken banister on the landing of the lodging house. Waxman carefully lights first Attenborough's face and then the broken rail. When Pinkie enters his room he finds that his authority is being challenged. Cubitt is relaxing on his bed, Spicer is counselling caution, and only Dallow offers unqualified support. But Dallow's fidelity is encouragement enough and Pinkie takes his razor to the instigator of rebellion: 'How do we make you safe, Spicer?' Cubitt is obliged to play the peacemaker. As Pinkie calls on Dallow to accompany him on a mission of enforcement and demonstrates his trust in his lieutenant by tossing him the razor, Boulting's camera dwells on Cubitt. He shakes his head and shows his apprehension about the position in which he finds himself: caught in no-man's-land between the potent Pinkie–Dallow alliance and the doomed Spicer.

We dissolve to Dallow's car pulling up outside Brewer's home on Brighton's Lewes Road. The impressive perspective set would suggest the tranquillity of leafy suburban living if it were not for the sinister presence of a freight train moving in shadow across the viaduct at the end of the street. The menacing shadow is echoed in the silhouettes of the two gangsters seen through Brewer's front door. Brewer's respectable home and concern for his sick wife establish him as a family man and emphasise the foreignness of violence in this setting. The protection racketeers will not respond to reason and show no compassion. Boulting builds tension, but the violence, when it comes, is sudden, short and decisive. Pinkie moves out of the shadows, raises his arm, and Brewer is left sprawling in his dressing gown against his bookmaker's board, clutching the gash in his cheek, and pathetically claiming that he has 'protection'. William Hartnell as Dallow shows his character's contempt for this suggestion by improvising a disdainful spit as the gangsters leave to the mournful sounds of a train whistle and a sick woman's coughing.

A substantial deviation from the shooting script follows. A short scene (set-ups 190 to 195) in Phil Corkery's office, where Ida places a bet on Black Boy and Phil receives a phone call from Colleoni, is cut. The missing scene's primary functions were to show Corkery's allegiance to Colleoni, and Ida setting off on her investigation of Fred's death, but their deletion is no great loss to the narrative. Ida's investigation is instead glimpsed in brief shots of her striding along the seafront and questioning Molly and Delia outside the Kings Court Hotel. The shot is cut into the film's next scene in which Pinkie pursues his own parallel crusade for recognition by audaciously going to visit Brighton's 'Governor' in his suite at one of the resort's opulent hotels.[41]

Colleoni has fired a warning shot across Pinkie's bows in the form of a letter sent after the attack on Brewer and now seems mildly amused by the young man's *chutzpah* in approaching him in person. The hotel receptionist, protective of a valued client, wants to know if Pinkie has an appointment. Satisfied, he allows access to Colleoni whose elevated status is emphasised by his vantage point on the balcony of the hotel lobby. To introduce Colleoni, Boulting reprises the shot of a man leaning over a rail that he had used for our first glimpse of Pinkie. The suggestion that the lowly Pinkie aspires to Colleoni's power and lifestyle is underlined by the boy's slow ascent of the hotel staircase, filmed in a long shot that draws attention to the smallness of the figure of Attenborough on the cavernous MGM sound stage. The shooting script makes the intention clear:

(Set-up) 211 Long Shot. The Hall. PINKIE enters. A shot from high up in the gallery shows the small shabby dwarfed figure. For the first time

14. *Challenging the law of the father: Attenborough and Charles Goldner at the Cosmopolitan.*

he looks totally inadequate [...] we watch the Boy's nervous progress across the entrance hall. People turn to look at him.

By the time Pinkie reaches his more powerful rival, Colleoni is lounging regally on a *chaise-longue*. While Charles Goldner as Colleoni affects a relaxed air, Attenborough keeps his body tautly erect, his hands clasped on the brim of his hat in front of him, like a petitioner approaching a monarch.[42] Indeed, the idea of a king's court is made explicit in the name of the hotel where Ida pursues her investigations in the intercut footage. The palatial character of Colleoni's Regency suite is clearly signalled by its elaborate decorative plasterwork, expensive *objets d'art*, and association with Napoleon III. Boulting further emphasises the gulf in power between the man and the boy by using a low angle camera for Goldner and a high angle for Attenborough. Colleoni is a man of taste, but it is also evident that he is a self-made man able to slip into the vernacular of the underworld when required. His description of Empress Eugenie as 'some foreign paloney' reveals his origins and, as he utters the words, Waxman contrives to place a shadow, like a razor scar across his cheek.

Colleoni is a significant figure in *Brighton Rock*'s allegorical schema.

Those commentators who are satisfied with Greene's implication that the character is based on Darby Sabini are really missing the point. Those who might note his resemblance to Al Capone, who died just before shooting began on the film, are getting closer. Those who point to the movie mogul Alexander Korda as a referent are closer still.[43] Colleoni is not a shadowy underworld figure, but a representative of the establishment. Green emphasises his status as a rich Jewish businessman and the intimate relationship between organised crime and the capitalist class. Living aloofly in protected luxury (he has not been on a race track 'for twenty years') and running an enterprise built on exploitation masquerading as 'protection', he represents the power of international capital that Greene held responsible for the social ills of the 1930s. 'You think you rule the world, don't ya?' asks Pinkie rhetorically.[44] The author had represented this malignant power before, notably in the enervated and enervating arms manufacturer, Sir Marcus, in *A Gun for Sale*; but while Sir Marcus is conventionally characterised as grasping and malevolent, Colleoni receives a more favourable gloss. He is given grace, charm and, above all, a paternalistic manner that positions Pinkie as a wayward son in the presence of a stern but benevolent father. Rather than employing the tough argot of a hoodlum, Colleoni addresses Pinkie as if he were a priest counselling one of his flock, using the phrase 'my child', and calming the young gangster's bluster. This is clearly a mirroring of the exchange between innocence and experience in the scenes between Rose and Pinkie, but it is also an inversion of Pinkie's role. He is no longer the experienced one. Beyond this, it is tempting to place Colleoni within the blasphemous theological code that seems to be inscribed into the story. If Pinkie represents a fallen Christ in a fallen world, then Colleoni is cast as his spiritual father – the fallen God of the material world – just as Kite was Joseph, and Dallow eventually becomes Judas. Thus, *Brighton Rock* might be read as a taxing biblical anagram with a solution as elusive as the Spiritualist word puzzle that Ida tries to decode. Pinkie leaves the king's court defiant, but with Colleoni's warning not to try to intimidate Brewer and Corkery ringing in his ears.

TWO INTERROGATIONS

By 1934 the [Brighton] Criminal Investigation Department had increased to one Detective Inspector, four Detective Sergeants and twelve Detective Constables, and this year saw the provision of the first car for their exclusive use. (Gerald Baines, *History of Brighton Police*, 1967)

Brighton Rock is full of doublings, deliberate repetitions and echoes. There is, for instance, a series of threats to Fred, to Rose, to Spicer and then to Pinkie himself. Similarly, there is a series of investigations: by Pinkie, by Ida and also by Brighton police. These threats and investigations are a feature of the central section of the film.

In a scene which precedes Colleoni's warning to Pinkie'in the shooting script, but follows it in the final cut, Ida continues her investigation of Fred's death at Snow's where, fortuitously, her waitress is Rose. Ida reveals her own brand of menace when she grabs Rose by the wrist and keeps her at the table. Scared, Rose inadvertently gives Fred's avenger a vital clue when she reveals that the man who left Kolley Kibber's card drank bottled beer. Greene's script gently mocks the conventions of Jacobean revenge drama by introducing Fred's ghostly voice declaring his aversion to that particular tipple. The hideous cackle that Ida gives in response plays against our over-identification with her character. On Ida's departure, Rose scuttles off to warn Pinkie, earning a disapproving look from the stern restaurant manageress (Daphne Newton). However, as Pinkie is at the Cosmopolitan, the increasingly anxious Spicer receives Rose's call. The close-up that Boulting gives us is meant to reveal 'how near he is to breaking'.[45] Meanwhile Pinkie, on leaving the Cosmopolitan, is picked up by the police, perhaps as a favour to Colleoni. The boy's pride is pumped up and he quips that a sergeant should be sent for him next time. As the police car pulls away we see a worried Spicer watching it depart.

Boulting dissolves to the cap badge of the police inspector (Campbell Copelin) who has sent for Pinkie. The Inspector's military moustache suggests a man who expects to be obeyed, but Pinkie is more relaxed than he was with Colleoni. His jacket is unbuttoned, his thumbs are in his pockets, and his hat sits at a jaunty angle on the back of his head. He seems to know where the real power in Brighton lies and it is at the Cosmopolitan Hotel rather than police headquarters. The closeness of the policeman to the Godfather of Brighton is subtly indicated by a mirroring of behaviour. Both offer the abstemious Pinkie something he refuses (a drink, a cigarette) and both address him while gazing out of a window. Although the Inspector purports to be even-handed in his treatment of the two gangsters, he assures Pinkie that it is Colleoni who will have the alibis. The boy is warned to 'clear out of Brighton' because he is not big enough for 'the filthy racket' he is in. Pinkie is unfazed. He acknowledges the 'valuable advice', but considers he is 'too young to retire'. He finds satisfaction in the notice on the charge room board that seeks information on a man found drowned. As he leaves the room, Greene's novel tells us, he trails 'the clouds of his own glory after him', but Greene's screenplay undercuts his cocky exit by having him come face to face with his Nemesis, Ida, who has come to share her suspicions about Fred's death with the police. Both register unease as they pass in the narrow corridor, as if realising that their lives are set on a collision course.

Ida's interview with the Inspector is another of the film's mirrorings, but this time the camera favours Ida during the dialogue, and it is she who has her back to the Inspector as she pores over the pathologist's report on Fred. Baddeley extracts full comic value from the list of Fred's bodily afflictions. The Inspector, a man used to having his judgements respected, finds his patronising assurances rebuffed by Ida, who, in turn, fails to convince him to take her suspicions seriously. She leaves, like Pinkie, with a statement of independence and defiance: 'I believe in right and justice and I'm going to see that it's done.'

ON THE PROM (AND UNDER THE PIER)

Further entertainment was provided by Jack Sheppard's pierrots, a group who performed on a covered open-air stage with a proscenium arch, on the lower promenade to the east of the Palace Pier. (Leonard Goldman, *Oh What a Lovely Shore*, 1996)

The paths of Ida and Pinkie inadvertently cross again in the next scene when the boy meets Rose at the sparsely-attended pierrot concert on Brighton's seafront.[46] Rose injudiciously reveals that she left a message for Pinkie with someone who sounded like the man who left the card at Snow's. Pinkie's reaction is to grab her wrist, just as Ida did in the restaurant. Again, this is part of the film's obsessive repetition of gestures, situations and shots. When Pinkie releases his grip, Rose gingerly rubs the spot is as if remembering the earlier bruise inflicted. Rose is questioned about the woman who questioned her. It appears the woman was not their kind – meaning perhaps that she was not a Roman Catholic or that she was neither innocent nor damned – and that she had a distinctive laugh. At that moment the laugh comes from the troupe of pierrots and Rose and Pinkie are united in stunned and fearful recognition. They rise from their deck chairs and the shock of recognition passes like an electrical relay to Ida. Like the trouper she is, she continues to sing.[47]

Now Ida Arnold is my name, good-hearted Ida's me,
The boys say I am just the type to take upon a spree.
I'll meet you any night you like and have a glass of port,
And if you're hen-pecked you'll agree that Ida is a sport.

Although the conversation between Pinkie and Rose is present in both Greene's novel and Rattigan's treatment, the venue is an innovation of the screenplay. The novel places the conversation in Peacehaven, the treatment on the Palace Pier. The relocation to the pierrot enclosure gives Boulting the opportunity to film in a more expansive setting which emphasises the depth of field and allows him to watch the couple picking their way through the rows of deck chairs as they leave.

Boulting's concealed camera picks out Pinkie and Rose as they emerge on the promenade near the Palace Pier. Rose makes a beeline for the street photographer's kiosk where the camera tracks her as she studies the display of photographs taken that day. To Pinkie's horror, she identifies a photo of Spicer as the man who left the card at Snow's. Rose's urgent desire to view the photographs is unmotivated and the appearance of Spicer's image comes as a shock to the viewer. However, this is a consequence of the editing process and was not the original intention. In the shooting script, street photography is a recurrent theme. After Pinkie is taken to the police station and the camera settles on Spicer, for instance, it was to follow his progress on to the pier where he is snapped by an opportunist commercial photographer:

(Set-up) 237. MS. Exterior Pier. SPICER hurries down into the eye of a street camera. We PAN with him.

238. Reversed and twisted as though in the lens of a camera – a shoulder follows.

VOICE: Take a card, sir?

239. MS. SPICER. Moves straight towards centre of picture. A hand with a card in it is large in the foreground. Spicer's body moves straight into camera and blacks out frame.

It is a brief but significant sequence, not only in preparing us for Rose's discovery at the kiosk, but also in the way in which the photographer's card is used to refer back to the one Spicer left at Snow's. As the screenplay informs us, the situation is 'reversed and twisted': the leaver of one card becomes the recipient of another, with fatal consequences. The 'eye' of the camera acts as intermediary for Rose's identification of the card leaver.[48] It is a beautifully conceived

15 and 16. *Gripping stuff: An example of the repetition of actions in* Brighton Rock. *Ida and Pinkie grasping Rose's wrist.*

moment and, in its irony and suggestion of poetic justice, fits neatly into *Brighton Rock*'s grand design. Its loss in the pursuit of a shorter running time is unfortunate but not as damaging as the deletion of the scene that would have explained Rose's eagerness to visit the photographer's kiosk.

The missing scene would have followed the one in the pierrot enclosure, and would have found Pinkie and Rose under the pier where 'the
piles rise like the pillars of a cathedral'.[49] The shooting script describes the
two figures sitting against one of the piles, facing in different directions.
Characteristically, Rose views the sea 'with the sunlight flowing upon it',
while Pinkie's vision takes in 'the rows of booths under the promenade,
the empty cigarette cartons and the waste-paper washed up like a dirty
line on the bath'.[50] From the pier above wafts the sound of the tune that
the couple heard in the dance hall, 'More Than Ever'. The music blends
with the waves breaking on the beach. Pinkie dismisses Rose's suggestion
that he might be scared of something and, as the camera creeps in to hold
them in a tight two shot, they begin to talk about their shared origins
and religion:

PINKIE: Where's home?

ROSE: Nelson Place. She's never lived there.

PINKIE: Who?

ROSE: That woman who keeps asking questions.

PINKIE: We can't all have been born in Nelson Place.

ROSE: Were you born there? There were Browns in Nelson Place– they
were Romans too.

PINKIE: Me? 'Course not. In that slum?[51]

ROSE: I'm glad you're a Roman too. You can see she doesn't believe
anything.

PINKIE: I don't take much stock in religion. You don't need to think
of it – not before you die.

ROSE: You might die sudden, Pinkie.

PINKIE: You know what they say: 'between the stirrup and the ground
he something sought and something found'.[52]

ROSE: Mercy.

PINKIE: That's right – Mercy.

ROSE: It would be awful though if they didn't give you time. That's
what I always pray, that I don't die sudden.

PINKIE: When I was a kid I thought I'd like to become a priest.
(derisively) They used to preach to us about love. 'God so loved
the world ...'

ROSE: I don't see what's wrong with love.

PINKIE: No. No. I used to watch it. I used to watch it Saturday nights.
There were five of us in a room ... When they remembered they
sent us outside into the street – mostly they didn't bother.

After a lengthy pause, Pinkie catches Rose looking at him and is vexed at being the object of her gaze. She reacts indignantly and displays a new facet of her personality. 'I'm not that dumb,' she assures him. 'I believe if it wasn't for that card I found you wouldn't ... ' For a moment, the power relationship between the two is overturned. Pinkie is suddenly scared and tries to reassure Rose that, although he has 'worries', they 'suit each other'. Thus the scene below the pier becomes a reversal of the earlier scene on the pier. Instead of the threat of vitriol, Pinkie fights his revulsion at physical contact to touch her hand and even to offer a kiss, but he is saved from having to carry it through by the interruption of the beach photographer who offers to take their photo. While Rose smiles for the camera, Pinkie covers his face and angrily tells the shutterbug to 'clear out'. The couple scramble up towards the promenade, where we see them emerge in the film's final cut. For the sake of continuity, however, the second part of Rose's exclamation on spotting the photographer's kiosk – 'Oh look, that's where we would have been stuck up' – is trimmed.

The deletion of the scene under the pier might seem understandable: it is talky, static, repeats elements of the dialogue in the dance-hall scene, does nothing to advance the action, and presents a challenge to the censor in Pinkie's description of Saturday nights. It is not even necessary for the comprehension of the plot and its loss poses only minor continuity problems. Nevertheless, the excising of this scene robs the film of some of its depth of characterisation, the back-story of its protagonist and, equally importantly for Greene, its theological core. Its removal might do nothing to harm *Brighton Rock* as a thriller (it might even enhance it by speeding up the action), but it diminishes the film as social drama and as a sensitive adaptation of Greene's novel. Our understanding of Pinkie is impoverished by being denied knowledge of 'the hell that lay about him in his infancy'. His status as a fallen angel – the delinquent who once wanted to be a priest – is obscured. The scene is the difference between an 'entertainment' and something of greater spiritual and intellectual weight. Even Greene, someone well versed in the requirements of popular film-making and philosophical about the need for simplification and pace, must have winced to see it on the cutting-room floor – snatched away mercilessly between the stirrup of production and the ground of the final cut. Peter Graham Scott is sure that the scene was included in his edit of the picture and must have been excised at some later date because 'some butcher decided the film was too long'.[53]

In his original treatment, Rattigan certainly felt there was a need to offer an explanation of Pinkie's character and apportion blame for his condition. He uses the gap between Pinkie's departure from the police Inspector's office and Ida's arrival to explore the issue:

> The Inspector speculates a moment with his subordinate on the boy's character. How is society responsible for turning out anything quite so vile as that? He knows about the boy's background, his life in the slums, his relationship with the gangster Kite. Sociologically there is an explanation for the type to which to which this boy belongs, but not for this specimen himself. Society must take some of the blame, but not all of it. A shared part of the blame seems to attach itself to the boy's creator.
>
> The detective, a kindly soul, disagrees. There is some good in every mother's son. It only needs to be discovered, encouraged and brought out. Perhaps the love of a good woman.

Greene might have approved of the Inspector's sentiments, but the detective's home-spun philosophising would have been anathema to a writer who was more interested in the burden of original sin and the possibilities of redemption than in the cultivation of the good within us all.

Despite the best efforts of Rattigan and Greene, the film can ultimately find no way to represent the social well-springs of Pinkie's misanthropy and we are left to conclude that he is a natural-born monster. His monstrosity is clearly evident in the scene in Spicer's bedroom. Boulting dissolves into the scene from a close-up of Spicer's photograph on the kiosk display and Rose's voiceover – 'and you said he was dead' – to another image of Spicer, prostrate on his bed, the twitch of his eye evincing his troubled dreams.[54] Pinkie hovers above him like a vulture waiting for carrion, his forefinger and thumb working against each other, itching to feel a razor between them. He chides Spicer about the message from Rose which he failed to deliver. 'You're too old for this life,' the boy tells him and turns away to the window, just as the authority figures Colleoni and the Inspector had done. As he tells the sweating Spicer that he must 'disappear', he is twisting his cat's cradle and staring into the Brighton night. In the shooting script, he squashes a fly against the windowpane in anticipation of what he will do to Spicer, but Boulting abandons that idea in favour of something more subtle. Waxman supplies him with an ethereal image of Pinkie's face reflected in the glass and suggesting exactly the kind of duplicity that he is practising with Spicer. The boy is literally two-faced as he reassuringly advises Spicer to take a holiday and then describes him as 'a pal I can trust'.[55] The ageing man nestles into a fool's paradise as the boy departs with an ironic 'Don't worry, I'll fix everything', and proceeds to set up an attack on Spicer by Colleoni's boys. As Attenborough sets up the hit, Waxman lights him from below, emphasising his satanic aspect. The light glistens on his Brylcreemed hair, slick and slippery like the boy himself.[56]

A DAY AT THE RACES

> If a thief or pickpocket was seen on a course a Sabini man would whiten the palm of his hand with chalk and greet the thief with a supposed-to-be 'Hello'. In doing so he would slap the thief on the shoulder, just like a long-lost friend. The whitened hand-mark would identify him to the law. (Billy Hill, *Boss of Britain's Underworld*, 1955)

Shot almost entirely on location, the scenes at the race-course form the centrepiece of *Brighton Rock*. Much of the credit for their success must go to production manager Gerry Bryant who put his documentary experience to good use in directing the second unit footage of the race won by Ida's fancy, Black Boy. Hans May's lively score also helps to capture the excitement of the occasion. In the spirit of the novel, the Boultings use the iconography of the race meeting to evoke *Brighton Rock*'s religious themes. An evangelist with a sandwich board (Norman Watson) proclaims 'The Wages of Sin' before breaking his sign over the head of one of Colleoni's razormen. The numerals of the winning horses arise in their frame like hymn numbers at a Sunday service, and the rituals of horse-race betting begin to resemble perverse devotions presided over by a priesthood of tick-tack men.

As Ida collects her winnings, she lets out a cackle that again alerts Pinkie to her presence, but he is a boy on a mission: dealing with Spicer. He puns on the 'peace' he hopes is in store for the oldest member of his mob, before giving him a Judas handshake and clapping him on the shoulder as a signal to Colleoni's thugs to do their worst. As they close in, Spicer sees he is cornered and his twitch becomes exaggerated, just as Fred's had when he was being hunted. The slashing of Spicer is captured in long shot from a high angle, as if we are being offered a morally elevated position, before we are plunged back into the mêlée. We witness Spicer's pain and then Pinkie's as he staggers into frame, his hand pressed against his bleeding cheek, crying out in shock and humiliation, just as Brewer had when Pinkie held the razor. Again, there is a symmetry of action and emotion: the perpetrator becomes the victim, the betrayer becomes the betrayed. Pinkie's response to the attack is flight rather than fight. The camera looks down on him as he rolls on the ground and seeks the opportunity to make a run for it. In Greene's novel, he is saved from further injury by the arrival of the police but, although the 'bogies' do eventually disperse Colleoni's gang in the film, it is the earlier intervention by bookies, punters and the evangelist that helps to rescue Pinkie and Spicer. The Boultings' crowd does not scatter 'at the first sign of trouble' as Greene's did, but act in the way the experience of war has taught them to act: as a concerned and supportive populace.[57] They get stuck in, and the ensuing rough and tumble offers the Boultings plenty of opportunities to picture Mickey Woods' Tough Guys Unlimited stunt team trading punches.

Pinkie has narrowly escaped further damage from the razor and, his castration fears reawakened, he eventually finds sanctuary in the basement of Snow's where his wounds are tended by Rose. Here he recasts her in a comforting maternal role, his ministering angel. Superficially, it is a tender moment – Pinkie even kisses Rose for the first time – but the tenderness conceals the fear and tension that grips them. As they hide in their subterranean bunker, Ida is snooping upstairs. The novel also makes clear that romantic thoughts are far from Pinkie's mind:

> He hated her as he hated Spicer and it made him circumspect; he pressed her breasts awkwardly under his palms, with a grim opportunist pretence of another man's passion, and thought: it wouldn't be so bad if she was more dolled up, a bit of paint and henna, but this – the cheapest, youngest, least experienced skirt in all Brighton – to have *me* in her power.[58]

Pinkie's awkward groping was never likely to make it to the shooting script, but Greene and Roy Boulting did try to establish Rose's virginity before the offending line – 'Pinkie, you're my first. I'm glad. I love you' – was excised. In fact, the scene has been extensively rewritten. In the shooting script, the scene begins in the alleyway at the side of Snow's where Pinkie presses his face, 'bloody and unkempt', against the window.[59] It is likely that this sequence was filmed as stills of Attenborough's bloodied face seen through the wet glass survive. But there is no trace of the original dialogue in which Pinkie tells Rose:

'I can't go out like this. I got to be respectable.' Perhaps it was feared that this level of irony might provoke laughs and break the mood of the scene.

SPICER'S FALL

Hurled headlong flaming from th' Ethereal Sky
With hideous ruin and combustion down
To bottomless perdition, there to dwell
In Adamantine Chains and penal Fire ...
(John Milton, *Paradise Lost*, 1: 45–8)

The clock is showing 6.15 as a disconsolate Pinkie arrives back at his lodgings, the camera rising to meet him as he approaches the stairs. Cubitt, chewing on an apple, intercepts him. As Pinkie pauses on the stairs, he tries unsuccessfully to keep his slashed cheek turned away. The camera shoots from a low angle below Cubitt's shoulder, and Waxman directs his key light at Pinkie's unblemished cheek, leaving the upper portion of his face in shadow. It is a striking, *noir*-ish composition. Cubitt informs Pinkie that his lawyer, Prewitt, has been looking for him. The spiv voices a disliking for the lawyer, and the contrast between the two men is evident from the moment we see Prewitt's sinister shadow through the glass of the front door.[60] While Cubitt represents a young straight-talking Britain living by its wits, Prewitt exudes the shabby gentility of a country gone to seed. He makes his entrance like a Shakespearean actor, even quoting Macbeth, and his constant references to 'the bard' and his contemporaries allude to the characteristics which *Brighton Rock* shares with Jacobean tragedy. Cubitt can't stand the fellow's 'chat', loathes his pretensions and no doubt deplores his taste in clothes. As he watches Pinkie's 'brief' ascend the stairs, the shooting script tells us that Cubitt is 'torn betwixt the emotions of disgust and perplexity. He forms the word "shit" with his mouth. We hear only a snort.'[61] Everything about the figure of Prewitt is antiquated, from the pinches of snuff he takes to the pince-nez that perches on his nose. If Cubitt is a modish fashion victim, Prewitt's attire looks as if it was bought when he was a young lawyer at the turn of the century. Harcourt Williams's portrayal is flawless, capturing the smallest nuance of an unprincipled character trapped in a loveless marriage, haunted by a sense of underachievement, and driven by avarice. Prewitt is a man reduced to using his legal knowledge to

17. *The broken banister: Dallow watches Pinkie push Spicer to his death.*

facilitate the ambition of a teenage gangster. Alcohol and disillusion
have long blunted his own. For Prewitt, the path to salvation is steep:
'the stairs are hard to climb'.

As Prewitt enters Pinkie's room the boy is busy in the foreground
spinning his web of string. He means to ensnare Rose by marrying
her to prevent her giving evidence against him. This is to be strictly
a marriage of convenience; it cannot be 'a real marriage, not like when
the priest says it'. Pinkie's cynical approach to matrimony is reflected
in Prewitt's own dismissal of his silver wedding: 'may the devil take
her first'. The lawyer is searching the wash stand for his fee when
Dallow enters with the revelation that Spicer is still alive. Attenborough
emphasises the boy's surprise by, back to camera, jerking his head round
as the shock registers. He quickly crosses the landing to confirm Spicer's
survival, simultaneously plotting another attempt on the life of the man
he sees as the weakest link in his organisation. Hans May's score evokes
Pinkie's shift of mood from shocked panic to homicidal calculation with
a swift change of pace by the strings as he checks the state of the banister before going into Spicer's room. The camera keeps the broken
banister in the foreground as Spicer backs towards it.

In his novel, Greene avoids describing the murder of Spicer, as he
does the murder of Fred. He 'cuts away' from the confrontation in

Spicer's room to Ida's confrontation of Rose at Snow's, and then back to Pinkie looking down at Spicer's broken body in the hallway at Frank's. The conventions of the film thriller, however, demand that the murder be seen, and Greene and the Boultings turn it into one of this film's most memorable moments. The scene's cinematography is a showcase for the talents of Waxman and his camera operator, Gil Taylor. It is also a triumph for Peter Graham Scott whose editing is as sharp as the razor that laced Pinkie. All are helped, however, by the precision of the Boultings' conception of the sequence. Shot sequences and camera angles are explicitly specified in the shooting script, as we can see from the extract below. It follows the close-up/reverse close-up sequence before Pinkie says goodbye to Spicer and offers him a handshake as he had done at the race-course.

> (Set-up) 347 CU Pinkie's feet. His left foot goes back and then he shoots it forward with terrible force against Spicer's shins (dummy legs).
>
> 348 CU Spicer. His face contorts with agony as he comes forward in an involuntary movement.
>
> 349 CU Pinkie. Spicer's head and shoulders come forward into frame towards Pinkie. Pinkie's left hand comes up and thrusts him sharply against the banister rail.
>
> 350 CU Spicer's face. It fills the screen. His mouth opened in a scream, his eyes wide. The face goes back with the thrust.
>
> 351 Medium CU. Banisters, low angle. Spicer breaks through the broken rail and hurtles down past CAMERA.
>
> 352 Long Shot from above landing shooting down through the broken rail to hall below. Spicer's body (dummy) falls. We see it spread-eagled below in the hall. Pinkie steps forward to the gap and looks down. We shoot over his head.

It is remarkable how closely the final edit sticks to the original conception of this montage sequence, but the Boultings and their camera crew also incorporate some inspired improvisations. As Spicer's body falls it breaks the gas mantle and flames spew out of the fitting, powerfully evoking the idea of hell-fire. Somehow, Taylor captures the impact of Spicer's head as it hits the floor, and finally Scott cuts to the sonorous effect on the hall's grandfather clock as it shakes free the newspapers clinging to its top. Spicer's fall is transformed into a minor cataclysm, but Waxman has yet to reveal his most stunning composition: the low-angle shot of Pinkie with Spicer's body reflected in the skylight above him as he very deliberately remarks, 'these banisters

18. *Cat's cradle: Pinkie discusses the finer points of law with his 'brief'*
(Harcourt Williams).

have needed mending for a long while'. The commotion brings the
blind Frank out of his workroom, the cloud of steam from his clothes
press adding to the impression of hellishness created by the burning gas
fitting. Thus murder is juxtaposed with the presence of a sightless man
as it was in the case of Fred's death. And while Frank cannot see, the
witnesses pretend not to have seen. Dallow acts as the loyal lieutenant
and Prewitt's attack of moral indignation quickly gives way to practical advice on the covering up of the crime. He has clearly had years
of experience in the manufacture of false stories. In any case, Pinkie's
will is not to be resisted. He is determined to demonstrate that, unlike
his victim, he is not 'milky'. His fear and desperation is replaced by a
satanic confidence as he takes command of the situation, barking orders
at the others as they cleanse the crime scene of incriminating elements.
His suitcase and bowler follow the unfortunate Spicer to the hard floor
of the hall, and Pinkie decrees that Cubitt, who was too fond of Spicer
for his own good, is to be given the same account of his death as 'the
bogies'. Pinkie makes coolly for the front door to establish an alibi
with Rose. He is 'going courting', an act which, for him, is the moral
equivalent of the murder of a friend.

The sequence is remarkable not only for the quality of its cinematography, acting and direction, but also for its evacuation of conventional morality and its mood of unredeemed cynicism. The mood is perfectly captured by Pinkie's suggestion that the sending of a card of condolence to Spicer's relatives would show 'proper feeling'. Showing and feeling are poles apart in this scene. It constantly draws attention to the yawning discrepancy between what its characters say and how they think and act, and, in the intensity of its *mise-en-scène*, it begins to suggest that venality and self-interest are universal traits of our fallen world. Moreover, in the way it uses an act of murder to showcase directorial talent and cinematographic skill, it anticipates the development of a horror cinema in which graphic killings are treated like production numbers in a musical. If there were nothing else of merit in *Brighton Rock*, this sequence would still make it a film worthy of serious attention.

WEDDED BLISS

She belonged to him like a room or a chair. (*Brighton Rock*, p. 128)

Greene's screenplay ruthlessly jettisons his novel's preambles to the wedding of Pinkie and Rose: the proposal, the stag night at a road house, Rose's sacking from Snow's, her discovery of Spicer's death fall, and the purchase of her parents' consent to marriage. Instead, the film moves straight to the Register Office where Dallow picks his teeth and studies the notices cautioning against giving false information to the registrar. The warning signs are literally there right at the beginning of Rose's marriage. Taking a seat, Dallow waits with fellow witness Prewitt for the tardy bride as Pinkie paces backwards and forwards across the frame with the regularity of a windscreen wiper. The accomplices in murder and marriage each discourse on wedded bliss. Pinkie envies a priesthood that is able 'to keep away from all this'. Dallow confesses that marriage got on his nerves; while Prewitt quotes Hamlet's advice to Ophelia: 'If thou hast needs marry, marry a fool. Because wise men know well enough what monsters you make of them.' Misogyny hangs heavy in the air as Rose finally arrives, without her parents who, as the novel (but not the film) informs us, have accepted 15 guineas for their daughter's hand. She has been to church in search of a state of grace but has been no more successful at achieving it than the men who have been waiting for her.

As the wedding party shuffles into the next room for the ceremony, with Prewitt calling on God to forgive them, Boulting dissolves ironically to the mechanical bellringers in one of the pier's slot machines, 'The Cathedral of Notre Dame'. The inspiration comes from Rattigan, whose treatment had suggested the use of a similar machine depicting an execution to foreshadow Fred's death. Pinkie pulls Rose away from this commercial representation of her romantic cravings. His idea of a honeymoon is to saunter distractedly among the pintables and peep shows of his sacred pier. Slot machines are, after all, the stock-in-trade of the Kite gang. Fate, however, draws Rose's attention to a recording booth, just as it had to the photographer's kiosk. She wants a record of her husband's voice to play on a borrowed gramophone if he is away. Pinkie cannot resist the infernal invitation displayed on the machine to 'Make it a personal message', and to create a ticking time-bomb of misery within his marriage of convenience. The shooting of this brief, shocking scene is exemplary. Boulting maintains a sense of realism by having extras pass between the principal actors and the camera; and then Taylor cunningly frames Pinkie's recording of his message of hate. Attenborough's scarred face is in the left foreground, with the microphone extending serpentine across the upper right and Marsh's adoring gaze illuminating the lower half. As the message grows uglier, Taylor slowly zooms in until Marsh's seraphic expression fills the frame.[62] For scholars of Graham Greene it is, of course, tempting to regard the disc Pinkie cuts on the pier as an emblem of the sub-text of *Brighton Rock*: the declaration of the author's own misanthropy (or misogyny), waiting to be discovered.

In Greene's novel, the happy couple spend their first married evening at the pictures, with Pinkie 'slumped grimly in the three and sixpenny seat', contemplating the sexual demands that will be made on him. The film is a full-blown romance, and including the scene would have given the Boultings a delicious opportunity to satirise the falsehoods of romantic melodrama.[63] The screenplay misses another trick here, because the cinema Greene probably had in mind as the venue was the Associated British-owned Savoy, where the film of his novel would have its première. Instead, the film moves straight to Pinkie's own unsuccessful romantic gesture: his attempt to book into a suite at the Cosmopolitan Hotel.

Perhaps it is pride rather than romance that powers Pinkie as he marches past philanderers and potted palms to the reception desk. Rose wanders behind him in her one-and-only cotton frock and flat sandals, looking about her in wonderment and clutching the precious record of her master's voice. Like Joseph and Mary (or John Lodge and Margaret

Lockwood in *Bank Holiday*), Pinkie and Rose find there is no room at
this particular inn. Pinkie's money is clearly not as good as anyone's,
especially when the one is Colleoni. It was Colleoni who had observed
the boy's previous visit to the Cosmopolitan's reception, but this time
it is Corkery and Ida who scrutinise him from the balcony as he leaves
in disgust. Ida, who is spending her winnings on the man they came
from, is determined to save Rose, whether she wants it or not. And so
the campaign to rescue her soul is hatched over the chrome teapots and
bone china.[64] The combination of Ida's intuitive powers and Corkery's
inside knowledge allows the pierrot and the bookie to piece together the
likely scenarios of Hale and Spicer's deaths. Prewitt emerges as the key
to confirming Ida's suspicions, and the shooting script segues straight
into her visit to the crooked lawyer, but the film's final assembly takes
us first to the wedding party in Frank's kitchen.

Brighton Rock's cynicism towards marriage is maintained in the first
shot of the wedding celebrations: a pan from Frank's sightless eyes to
his hand entwined with his wife's, and on to reveal that Judy is sitting
on Dallow's lap.[65] It is an eloquent evocation of marital infidelity. Across
the kitchen, Cubitt is sitting cross-legged on a side table like a jester at a
banquet. He is passing ribald comment on Pinkie's nuptials and spanking
the bottom of a doll that recalls the one Pinkie had mutilated in an
earlier scene.[66] A disapproving Pinkie arrives, framed in the doorway;
Malvolio to Cubitt's Feste. The young puritan is assailed by the same
gales of mocking laughter that followed Fred to his grave. The scene
seems to be designed to replay Pinkie's childhood trauma on witnessing
his parents copulating. The expressionist close-ups of Judy's gaping
mouth, and the doll calling 'Mama', not only quote earlier shots of Ida,
but express Pinkie's fear and loathing of female sexuality. In Freudian
terms, he is regressed to the pre-Oedipal phase of the 'oral' mother,
and experiences the need to reassert his post-Oedipal masculinity.
Thus the 'oral' shots are counterpointed by the jarring close-up of the
boy's glaring eyes and flaring nostrils as he turns his anger on Cubitt,
disclosing his role in Spicer's death and displaying his phallic power.
Dallow plays the peacemaker, framed between the antagonists like a
boxing referee, bow-tied and white-shirted.[67] Waxman's lighting makes
the anger on the actors' faces positively glow, but part of the tension is
defused by a clumsy edit from a close-up to two shot as Cubitt raises
his fist and Pinkie's hand goes to his razor.

Finally, Cubitt has had enough and, realising he is likely to be the
boy's next victim, quits the mob. Pinkie has won a wife but lost a

lieutenant; although Dallow remains loyal as long as no harm comes to Rose. The sequence is perfectly in keeping with the psychology of misogyny and sexual repression; Pinkie's anger is a sublimation of the disgust and anxiety provoked by the expectation of intercourse with his bride. It is a mechanism that has driven his ambition throughout his adolescence. Now, his anger assuaged, he climbs the stairs to face his own worst horror of all. Greene's novel describes the circumstances of the boy's lost virginity, but the film suffers from a touch of Breen phobia and draws a discreet veil over the proceedings. It is another opportunity missed. Instead we dissolve to Prewitt opening a box, which some might regard as a suitably subtle sexual metaphor.

THE TERMINATOR COMES TO CALL

[I]deas never changed, the world never moved: it lay there always, the ravaged and disputed territory between the two eternities. (*Brighton Rock*, p. 139)

The scene in which Ida interrogates Prewitt is one of the few Rattigan innovations to survive Greene's rewrite. In the novel, it is Pinkie who visits the lawyer, but Rattigan saw that the dipsomaniac Prewitt would be a soft touch for Ida in her investigations, and Greene saw the wisdom of the change, accepting many of Rattigan's amendments to his original dialogue. The result is an entertaining study in contrasting characters, as the domineering but maternal Ida hounds the crumbling ruin that is Prewitt. Ida, unseasonably encumbered in fox stole, gloves and another of her inexhaustible supply of ghastly hats, storms his office. Prewitt greets her with, 'Madam, I haven't had the pleasure', and here is at least part of his problem: his alcoholism, like Pinkie's misanthropy, has its origins in blocked sexuality.[68] The lawyer's refuge from a hostile world is a shabby office besieged by noise from shunting trains, his neighbour's dance-band music and complaints from his wife on the floor below.[69] He opines that he married beneath him, and this seems to have been continued in the physical arrangement of the couple's living conditions. Maudlin and dyspeptic, he shuffles between the potted aspidistra in the window and the roll-top desk against the cracked wall. On the wall, a photograph of happier days at a minor public school reminds him of the state of grace from which he has fallen. Pride, as we know, goes before a fall, but for Prewitt, 'Prideaux' comes after: it is the name on the deed box in which he keeps his Burgundy, and of the long-deceased client he invokes to convince others that he still has a viable legal practice. His fall is so profound that he now carries 'the secrets of the sewer', and concurs with Mephistopheles that he already inhabits a hell on earth. His room becomes a confessional and Ida is cast as his priest, the role Greene originally intended for Pinkie. But if she is to be a priest, Ida chooses to be a Jesuit inquisitor. She is constantly in Prewitt's face, intruding into the frame, until he eventually drops his guard like his teacup and is left to pick up the pieces. Prewitt is clearly a prey to 'the worst sin': despair.

Back at Frank's, Rose turns sleepily to cuddle her new husband, only to find that he has 'gone out without his breakfast'. She has been woken by the considerate Judy with a cup of tea and a promise of a gramophone on which to play Pinkie's recording. Judy is replaced by Dallow, who clearly displays paternal concern for a 'good kid'. Rose, however, remains under the spell of evil. 'You're his friend, aren't you?' she sighs, as if addressing a disciple of the Messiah, 'I wish I was.' She knows that Pinkie is one of the damned, and probably means her harm, but she is intoxicated by him and embraces her fate with equanimity. It is her self-imposed role to endure.

Enter Ida, masquerading as Rose's mother, and bringing with her a distinctly militant maternalism wrapped in righteousness. 'I'm here to see justice done,' she announces to the horrified Rose, who backs into a corner as Ida advances. Rose senses the monstrosity of a figure who usurps the Lord's prerogative and tries to take responsibility for her salvation. A female priest is monstrous enough, but a priestly pierrot? Ida's notion of saving Rose centres on her removal from physical harm – 'Your life's in danger' – but for Rose, salvation is a process for the soul rather than the body – 'I wouldn't want to be saved if he was lost'. The clash of cultures and world-views represented by the two women is expressed visually in the tight shot/reverse shot editing pattern adopted by Boulting and Scott. The sequence contains the key debate of the film, as Rose tries to convince Ida that 'People change, repent', and Ida, taking herself as an example, asserts the immutability of human nature: 'I'm like those sticks of rock – bite all the way down, they still read "Brighton".'

As Pinkie returns, he is met by Judy, the housemother, who continues the taunting of the previous evening by telling him that Rose's mother is waiting to kiss him. The association of motherhood and eroticism hardly has time to provoke nausea in Pinkie before he hears Ida starting to leave. In a phrase now resonant of *The Terminator* (1984), she assures Rose 'I'll be back'. Pinkie hides as, in the words of the shooting script, 'she sails furiously down the stairs'.[70] Pinkie knows that Rose is lying when she maintains the fiction of a visit from her mother, and he becomes even more suspicious than usual: eyes darting around in search of anything out of place. He spies the love letter Rose had written to him while he was at the wedding celebrations. Rose, meanwhile, combs her hair – a reminder of the locks Pinkie pulled from the fairground doll – and the diegetic sounds of a baby crying, woven around May's score, warn the boy of the fate in store if he succumbs to love. As Pinkie reads, Rose watches with excited eyes, hoping like some fisher of men that he will take her bait. Greene clearly intends the love note to be the inverted equivalent of Pinkie's recording. Each will have a different function from the one expected by its creator. Each message is the obverse of what its recipient wants to know. 'You gave me the gramophone record. I wanted to give you something too,' she tells him. And she has; but we can tell from his false grin that it is a warning and a further opportunity for evil.

When Rose is safely out of the room, Pinkie expresses his rage and disgust by slamming the window shut, muffling the baby's mewling. In the moment that follows, Boulting encourages Attenborough silently to express the flow of thoughts and emotions running through Pinkie's mind, and to resolve them by flinging his hat to the floor. Dallow is his last ally, but when Pinkie tries to tell him of Rose's deceitfulness and the consequences that must follow, it is evident that Dallow's loyalties have shifted. Dallow has faith in love and 'would trust that kid all the way'. The boy, on the other hand, values love only if it ensures his own security. Love is just another lever of power that might be pulled to bring compliance with a bogus suicide pact and a resultant peace (pax) from anxiety.[71]

Although in the novel it is the disgruntled Cubitt who supplies information to Ida, the role of informer has already been taken by Prewitt in the film, and Cubitt is allowed quietly to take the train to London. Instead of interrogating Cubitt, Ida marches Prewitt down to the police station, but, as the next short scene reveals, she cannot make him give evidence against Pinkie.[72] The scene may perhaps seem a little superfluous, but it provides the technical function of allowing an easier transition between two scenes in Pinkie's bedroom taking place at different times, and the discursive function of illustrating one of *Brighton Rock*'s central themes: the difference between a human justice based on right and wrong, and a divine justice linked to ideas of good and evil. Ida's futile attempt to persuade Prewitt to incriminate his client demonstrates the imperfections and arbitrariness of human justice, and the way 'right' and 'wrong' are contingent on partiality, self-interest and greed.

THE WORST SIN

PINKIE: I'd feel a stranger away from here. I suppose I'm real Brighton.
(*Brighton Rock*, shooting script, set-up 472 [deleted from the film])

A view of Brighton seafront and a theatrical clap of thunder herald the last act of *Brighton Rock*. Back at Frank's, Pinkie lies brooding over a letter we assume to be the one from Rose until he reveals to Dallow that it is an offer from Colleoni to buy out the Kite gang's financial interests in Brighton. Dallow is thrilled by the offer and is ready to decamp, but Pinkie is not so keen to leave the corner of purgatory he has made his own. The optimistic Dallow is a captive of spontaneity; he reacts to the moment and wallows in its pleasures. Pinkie, by contrast, is a pessimist who, like a chess player, has to plan many moves ahead to avoid disaster. The differences between the pair are becoming more marked as the mood created by the gloomy *mise-en-scène* and the ominous murmurings of the score grows steadily darker. Between the peels of thunder, the actors are filmed from low angles with high contrast lighting casting dark shadows in classic *noir* fashion. Dallow picks his nails and Pinkie twists his string as the tension slowly builds.

Noticing the gramophone, Pinkie starts searching for his recording; 'evidence' that must be destroyed. Before he can completely smash it, however, he is interrupted by Rose's return. The shot is beautifully composed with the record concealed behind Pinkie's back in the left foreground, the beaming Rose centre frame in the background, and the washstand balancing the composition in the right foreground. When Dallow is called to the telephone, Pinkie grimly informs Rose that 'We're nearly through'. He plays on her dependency, feigning tenderness as he tells her that suicide might be the only way out and slipping the battered record under the bedclothes. Light glistens on the metallic surfaces of the record and bedstead, and on the tears that well in Carol Marsh's eyes as Boulting draws an emotionally powerful performance from her. She sobs that the despair represented by suicide is the worst of all mortal sins, and that it must not be contemplated. As Pinkie embraces her, Gil Taylor inches in to a tight and eloquent close-up of his face, its cold eyes still revealing his calculations for his next move. The mood is finally broken by a euphoric Dallow with the news that Pinkie's fears have turned out to be misplaced because Ida has failed to turn Prewitt and is leaving town.

At this point, the shooting script includes a scene (set-up 483) set inside the pierrot enclosure. It consists of a brief dialogue between Phil Corkery, who sits on a packing case smoking a cigar, and Ida, who is stowing away her props:

PHIL: I never known you leave a thing unfinished before, Ida.
IDA: I got a living to earn. The troupe goes on – I got to go on too. I don't like it, Phil, but I got to go.
PHIL: You certainly had 'em scared.
IDA: Didn't want to scare them. I wanted to ring that boy's neck.
PHIL: *She* wouldn't thank you.
IDA: I don't want thanks. I just want what's right, that's all.
PHIL: You're a terrible woman, Ida.

They agree to go for a goodbye drink in the Feathers 'where it all began', and the camera pans away down to where an old Kolley Kibber card is lying in the mud. It is probable that the scene was never filmed because Peter Graham Scott has no recollection of it. Its loss is not crucial to narrative comprehension – Dallow has already informed us that Ida is leaving Brighton – but, for Greene, it is a final chance to underline the foreignness of Ida to the culture shared by Pinkie and Rose. Her relationship to the 'real' Brighton, the one beyond the tourist gaze, is temporary and uncommitted. Ultimately, she is a stranger, not a local.[73] While Pinkie is Brighton rock in the adamantine sense, born and bred, Ida can never be more than the confectionery. Thus, she will never understand the true nature of the eternal struggle in which Pinkie and his bride are engaged.

THE WAGES OF SIN

> ... the will
> And high permission of all-ruling Heaven
> Left him at large to his own dark designs,
> That with reiterated crimes he might
> Heap on himself damnation, while he sought
> Evil to others, and enraged might see
> How all his malice served but to bring forth

> Infinite goodness, grace and mercy shown
> On Man by him seduced, but on himself
> Treble confusion, wrath and vengeance poured
> (John Milton, *Paradise Lost*, 1: 211–20)

The Four Feathers pub is no place for cowards. It is the meeting point of the hunters and the hunted; the venue for the pursuit to begin. On this night, Hale's hunter will become the quarry. The celebration for the salvation of Kite's gang is not all it seems. Invisible currents of deceit flow between the participants. Dallow, Judy and Rose are looking forward to going to 'the country', which is how Dallow regards the manufacturing city of Leicester. Pinkie is keeping his options open. He is not drinking. His hands nervously move loose change from one to the other as if he is counting pros and cons, or preparing to chance his future on the toss of a coin. But he is prepared: he has a gun in his pocket. Judy believes Dallow will take her away with him, and she symbolises their partnership by drinking from his glass. But Dallow is non-committal and withdraws the glass from her.

Any happy thoughts of the country are banished by the arrival of Ida with Corkery.[74] The sight of his Nemesis is enough to make up Pinkie's mind. He tells Dallow, in a voice loud enough for Ida to hear, that the country (in the sense of a more blessed place than the fallen world of Brighton) 'don't suit Rose and me', and that the end has come for them. Ironically, he intends Ida to be a witness to his 'suicide *pax*'. The optimistic Dallow advises him to 'never say die'; but Pinkie drops a heavy hint that death is exactly what he desires. In yet another of the film's mirrorings, he takes a drinking glass from Rose as Dallow had from Judy. The hopes of the two women go with the glasses. Dragging Rose from her bar stool, Pinkie elects to go for a walk in the rain. As he passes Ida, in a defiant gesture of phallic power, he pats the gun in his pocket, signalling his violent intentions and warning her not to intervene. Realising Pinkie's intentions, Ida urgently seeks the aid of Judy and Dallow, but only with the mention of the gun does Dallow appreciate the danger to Rose. He knows the penalties for being found in possession of a firearm, and that a professional criminal would carry the weapon only if he meant to use it. As the film has already established, Dallow is a man who believes in moderation and who has a soft spot for Rose. It is suddenly clear to him that Pinkie has gone too far and is now in breach of the codes of the underworld. He instructs the obedient Judy to 'fetch a bogy [policeman]', and, in an inversion

19. *Is that a gun in your pocket?: Pinkie, Corkery (George Carney), and Ida (Hermione Baddeley) at the Four Feathers.*

of the earlier pursuit of Hale, he leads an unlikely party of rescuers from the Feathers to the pier.

It is not difficult to guess where Pinkie will go. In the novel, Pinkie drives Rose to the cliffs at the symbolically named Peacehaven to stage her suicide, but the film follows Harvey's play in confining the action to Brighton. Outside the Feathers, when Rose had asked him if anything was wrong, he had replied, 'Everything – let's go on the Pier.' Suspended between two elements – the sky and the stygian sea – and the eternities of heaven and hell, the pier is Pinkie's favourite place of torments, his springboard to Hades. In the storm that rages at *Brighton Rock*'s conclusion, the metal structure becomes a kind of spiritual lightning rod, conducting the cosmic forces that will preside over the boy's demise. At the pier-head, beyond the Dante's Inferno ride, the boy gangster and his pubescent moll contemplate their mortality above the inky waters. Pinkie waves Rose's love letter and tells her that it is the end for both of them. Rose again battles with her Catholic conscience and the knowledge that suicide will bring inevitable damnation, but cannot allow her husband to die alone. He places the gun in her hand and assures her that 'It won't hurt', finally sealing the '*pax*' with a cold killer's kiss. Rose's tears mix with the raindrops as

20. *The worst sin: Pinkie tempts Rose to commit suicide.*

her face, sobbing in the ecstatic agony of martyrdom, fills the screen.
As her tormentor leaves her to take her own life, she stares at the gun
as if it were some dreadful apparition. Her hope is ebbing away, but,
as Boulting cuts away to her rescuers passing through the Palace of
Pleasures where her husband had recorded his message of hate, we
know that earthly salvation is at hand. Rose utters a prayer and lifts the
gun. Like some malevolent hypnotist, Pinkie watches with satisfaction
as the barrel reaches her temple, but before she can pull the trigger she
hears the rescue party running down the steps towards her. Pinkie's
spell is broken, and Rose, revolted by the revolver, tosses it into the
sea before its owner can retrieve it from her.

   Peter Wollen has argued that the endings of spiv films 'are often
where melodrama decisively triumphs over realism'.[75] *Brighton Rock* is
no exception. Pinkie's last moments are spent in abject panic as the
police corner him and his trusted lieutenant Dallow betrays him. As
he climbs the pier railings in terror and confusion, Boulting manages
to render him as an evil but ultimately pathetic figure: a wicked child
finally brought to book by the adult world for his crimes. He has
reverted to the mewling infant whose noise he shut his window to
muffle, and, as he tips over the edge, he even seems to utter a strangled
cry of 'mother'. His pride has gone by the time of his fall. Boulting

has robbed him of any vestigial glory that Greene might have deemed appropriate.[76] In Greene's novel, Pinkie's death is surrounded by a sense of tragedy, of the wilful rejection of redemptive opportunities, of the disabling power of evil. His death dive is preceded by 'the prowling pressure of pity': 'An enormous emotion beat on him, it was like something trying to get in, the pressure of gigantic wings against the glass.'[77] The film might have conveyed this idea with expressionistic flash cuts, but it settles, instead, for the safety of genre convention: the self-styled 'big shot' displaying the coward within and succumbing to righteous force. In part, the way the film conventionalises Pinkie's end is an accommodation to prevailing regimes of censorship. In the shooting script, as in the novel, Pinkie pulls out his bottle of vitriol to hurl defiantly at his persecutors, and a well aimed police truncheon shatters the phial and spills the acid over his face. Disfigured and in agony and despair, he then takes his own life:

(set-up) 518 CU Pinkie's face. The bottle comes up and he grasps the cork between his teeth. His eyes are aflame with hate.

519 CU The Policeman. He raises and throws his truncheon right across CAMERA.

520 CU Pinkie's face. The bottle is caught by the truncheon just as it is being taken away from the teeth. The contents spurt up into his eyes. He screams. The CAMERA pulls back. He stands there for a moment in desperate agony and then, doubled up and still screaming, he staggers to the rail, pulls himself over and drops into the sea.

The intended ending is more horrific, but also more powerful. There is the bitter irony of the tormentor destroyed by his own instrument of intimidation, the possibility of divine assistance in the policeman's marksmanship, the anticipation of the flames of hell as the acid burns, the pain that prevents the sinner seeking forgiveness between 'the stirrup and the ground', and the 'glory' of a damnation achieved by conscious sinning and ensured by suicide. In the final version, it is not too clear whether Pinkie has jumped for glory or, more likely, fallen by accident. Either way, he has been seen off by the forces of right represented by Ida. The only slight suggestion that those forces might not also represent good is the brief shot Boulting gives us from Pinkie's viewpoint of his pursuers leaning over the rail between the worlds of the living and the lost. Lit from below, the watching faces take on a satanic aspect, but only, perhaps, because they are illuminated by hellfire.

THE WORST HORROR

Man shall not quite be lost, but saved who will,
Yet not of will in him, but grace in me
(God in Milton's *Paradise Lost*, 3: 173–4)

The final scene of *Brighton Rock* is its most controversial. The novel ends
with Rose walking home to discover the proof of Pinkie's hate for her
when she plays the recording of his voice. Greene asks us to consider
the dreadful ironies consequent on the exercise of divine will: that the
gross sinner might be saved from damnation by mercy provoked by
the love of a good woman, whose reward is to face 'the worst horror
of all'. The film offers a lighter variation on this theme. Looking even
younger than her sixteen years, Rose sits on a convent bed, a child bride
attended by a bride of Christ. She is entirely unrepentant, rejecting
absolution and wishing that she had died and been damned with her
husband. The camera moves in to her tear-streaked face as she maintains
that Pinkie loved her and that neither Ida nor the sympathetic Mother
Superior – the profane and sacred sisters of mercy – knows anything
about love. As Rose indicates that she has proof of Pinkie's feelings,
Boulting cuts to a close-up of the gramophone that is waiting to play
the boy's message of hate. 'There is always hope,' the nun assures her
softly, 'it is the air that we breathe.' The 'appalling strangeness of the
mercy of God', it seems, is incomprehensible; and Rose unknowingly
demonstrates its effects when she plays her treasured recording. As she
moves towards the light of the window, as Pinkie, Colleoni and the
police Inspector had done before her, the needle sticks on the words 'I
love you'. The camera dollies in on the crucifix on the convent wall as
if to confirm both God's love and the strangeness of his mercy.[78]

The ending, as we have seen, owes much to Rattigan, who introduced
the trope of the faulty disc. In his treatment, Rose has been given
shelter by Ida and Corkery, and, after spending some days recovering
from Pinkie's death, she eventually gets round to playing his recording:
'The three gather round the machine to hear it. The recording is rough
and the needle scratches for some seconds before The Boy's voice is
audible. "I love you", it says hollowly, and then the needle sticks and
the record begins to repeat itself. "I love you ... I love you ... I love
you ... I love you." Corkery makes a move to lift the soundbox past
the scratch, but Ida restrains him, nodding towards Rose. Rose, her eyes
fixed in an unseeing stare on the ceiling, is listening in rapture.'[79]

21. The worst horror of all: Rose waits with the Mother Superior (Anna Steele) to play Pinkie's message of hate in the film's controversial and disputed last scene.

In a television interview in 1995, Roy Boulting disowned the ending, blaming the Secretary of the BBFC, Joseph Brooke Wilkinson, and claiming that he and Greene had fought for a scene based on the ending in the novel. Boulting even asserted that the ending had been reshot after completion of principal photography: 'That old boy [Brooke Wilkinson] – as if it was the last battle, the last rampart he would man – said "No! You've got to change it." It had to be done in one day, and the lighting was quite different from the rest of the film. It was a compromise, and I would have much preferred the earlier ending … '[80] However, the shooting script offers no corroboration to Roy's memory, and, twenty years before, brother John had clearly said of the ending: 'We wanted to maintain the horror without the brutality, the censors were not involved.'[81] Peter Graham Scott, who never liked the 'facile' ending, recalls that 'Graham had to be talked into it', but Greene himself maintained that the ending was the one specified in his own treatment.[82] This is confirmed by Judith Adamson, who has examined the manuscript held at the University of Texas, Austin. She reports that Greene specified that the scene 'must be done with complete realism from sentimentality', and was disappointed with the Boultings' use of the image of the crucified Christ and the casting of too young a woman for the Mother Superior role.[83] He believed that the ending of his novel was too bleak for a commercial film, and would go on to argue unsuccessfully for a happier ending to *The Third Man*.[84] In 1969 he was still prepared to defend the analgesic in the tail of *Brighton Rock*:

> I like the ending of the film and I am completely guilty. [...] I knew the distributors would not accept the ghastly ending of the book. I also knew that people would realise that one day Rose would move the needle beyond the crack and thus get the shock with which the book ends. The ghastly outcome was only delayed. It was the director's idea to pan up to the crucifix on the wall. This gave the impression that the needle stuck miraculously. Earlier in the film Pinkie tried to destroy the record but was interrupted by Rose. This explains the crack in the record. There is nothing miraculous about it.[85]

Of course it could be that divine will caused the crack to form at that particular place, just as it might be interpreted that the shot of the crucifix is, as John Boulting himself indicated, an ironic comment on an event with a perfectly rational explanation.[86] There is a pleasing ambiguity to the ending, but the fact remains that, in a reversal of the novel, it is Rose rather than Pinkie who has become the candidate for a demonstration of the 'appalling strangeness' of God's mercy.

FOUR
Release

CRITICAL VITRIOL

The normal boy likes excitement [...], but I doubt if he often copies
deliberately what he reads or sees on the films. He may imitate the
externals: the swaggering walk and the boastful methods of the fictional
gangster, but this influence does not go deeper. (Sir Harold Scott, Metropolitan Police Commissioner, *Scotland Yard*, London: André Deutsch,
1954, p. 68)

It is close to midnight on 8 January 1948. After three hours of queueing,
2,750 are packed into Brighton's Savoy cinema eagerly awaiting the
première of *Brighton Rock*. They are enjoying a stage show compered
by Richard Attenborough. Wylie Watson is on stage wise-cracking that
he had been afraid to return to Brighton lest he be arrested for theft.
The stolen property turns out to be two blades of race-course grass still
adhering to his shoe on his arrival in London.[1] Earlier in the evening,
Watson, together with John Boulting, Hermione Baddeley, Sheila Sim,
William Hartnell and Nigel Stock, had been welcomed at the railway
station with an announcement over the loudspeakers. The film's cast
had then been whisked off to an informal dinner attended by the Mayor,
Mayoress and the Chief Constable of Brighton as well as local celebrities
and the press. Richard Attenborough had gone direct to the reception
by car from Pinewood Studios.[2] Of the principal actors, only Carol
Marsh, who is making a film in France, is missing. The atmosphere is
convivial, but the event has been overshadowed by an extraordinary
attack on the film in one of the morning papers.

By and large, *Brighton Rock* had been given an encouraging reception
by the trade press after their screening the previous November. *The
Cinema* had described the film as 'vivid action entertainment for devotees
of strong drama', praising its 'realistic portrayal' of 'authentic Brighton
backgrounds', fine performances and 'forceful direction'.[3] Josh Billings

in *Kinematograph Weekly* had acknowledged its box-office potential, but had detected a slackness in the script and direction that meant the film 'only meets the best Hollywood gangster films half-way'.[4] Although there were some reservations, it looked as if *Brighton Rock* would prove a congenial confection; but there were also worrying signs that it might prove too tough for the taste of the times. The wedding of Princess Elizabeth seven weeks previously had encouraged a penchant for soft-centred entertainment, particularly among the numerically dominant female audience. Just prior to Christmas, for example, *The Cinema* had reviewed the recent and upcoming releases. Its anonymous studio correspondent felt obliged to take note of the views of his neighbour, 'Mrs. P.', one of those respectable, middle-aged women who 'at the mention of the word "spivs" firmly declares that she does not want to see films in which they are featured'. The correspondent felt obliged to remind himself that 'much as the long-haired artist in some of us would like to make rude gestures at the commercial interests and proceed to create sombre studies for the delectation of the intellectual, we are overlooking the needs of the harassed Mrs. P., who looks to the cinema for relaxation'.[5]

Concern for the sensibilities of Mrs P. was prominent in the assault on *Brighton Rock* launched by the *Daily Mirror* film critic, Reg Whitley, on the morning of the film's première. Condemning it as 'false, cheap, nasty sensationalism', Whitley asserted that 'no woman will want to see it' or allow her children to see it. Moreover, he believed that the film's 'ninety-two minutes of murder, brutality, beating-up' would create for foreign audiences an 'untrue picture of life in Britain' at a time when exports were the lifeline of the national economy.[6] Graham Greene was so affronted by Whitley's diatribe that he immediately penned a letter to the *Mirror*, defending the Boultings' attempts to incorporate the book's 'religious theme', blaming the BBFC for hampering their efforts, and pointing out that the film was never intended for children.[7]

Luckily, some of the damage done by the *Daily Mirror* had been repaired by the London evening papers by the time Boulting and the cast reached Brighton. Margaret Lane in the *Evening Standard* has pronounced *Brighton Rock* 'the best film that has appeared for many weeks', and suggested that, although the subject is sordid, the treatment is so true that the viewer begins to feel a kind of elation that lasts until the end.[8] The *Evening News*'s Jympson Harman not only suggested that the film was 'splendidly directed', 'ideally cast' and full of 'magnificent performances', but also went a long way towards soothing local doubts about the suitability of the subject for promoting the town with the headline: 'Brighton is now a film star'.

How much more enjoyable it makes a movie when you know the places where the story happens. 'Surely you recognised that tea shop, those deck chairs, that fun fair – and isn't that the part of the pier where you sat when we talked about settling down together?' You know just how the victim felt when he struggled up the hill to the station to make a get-away from the razor-gang. And wasn't he lucky to slip onto a passing bus towards the sea, past the theatre, through the Lanes with their antique shops, past the Pavilion and so on?[9]

It was the sort of cosy gentility, laced with (unintentional?) gallows humour that would have been at home in a contemporary production from Ealing Studios. However, it would prove difficult for other commentators to pause to appreciate the familiar pleasures of the film's Brighton backgrounds when they were preoccupied with the delinquency depicted so vividly in the foreground.

Two weeks before *Brighton Rock*'s première the Home Secretary, Scottish Secretary and the Minister of Education had appointed a committee to investigate the effects of attendance at the cinema on children under sixteen, with special reference to cinema clubs.[10] The concern was underlined in a New Year speech to the Incorporated Association of Headmasters by its Chairman, Dr P. T. Freeman, at London's County Hall. He described the cinema as 'one of our worst and most powerful enemies' which contributed 'very little towards giving the young a sense of values'.[11] This was a predictable view at a time when the number of adolescents being imprisoned had increased by 250 per cent since 1939, and it was a familiar one to the Boultings. From the day they received Greene's script for *Brighton Rock*, the BBC radio serial *Dick Barton – Special Agent* had been the focus of debates about the moral responsibilities of programme-makers and appropriate entertainment for the young.[12] The Boultings' own responses to questions from journalists about the wisdom of filming Greene's novel during the post-war crime wave had been to stress its efficacy as a modern morality tale: 'We are not so much concerned with the sadistic and brutal action of the story, as with the reasons for those acts. The boy gangster is revealed as an object of misery rather than glory.'[13] But such pieties would not spare their film from controversy at a time when law and order were high on the political agenda.

The questions from journalists had been prompted by the shooting

22. *Razorblade smile: Attenborough and Baddeley enjoy a friendly cup of tea off camera.*

of Alec d'Antiquis, a 'have-a-go hero' who had tried to prevent the
getaway of thieves robbing a pawnbroker in London's Charlotte Street.
The young men responsible had been tried at the Old Bailey while
filming on *Brighton Rock* took place at the race-course, and their execution coincided with the completion of the film. The state's revenge
had been a good deal swifter than Pinkie's. The case provoked a
police clamp-down on crime in the capital. The figures for indictable
crime were 50 per cent above the pre-war level; and the problem of
organised crime had been considered serious enough to warrant the
formation of a new undercover unit, 'the Ghost Squad' (although
the leading mobs were no mystery to a number of their police col-
leagues who benefited financially from their patronage). However,
in Parliament, a new, more liberal, Criminal Justice Bill was being
prepared in the face of opposition from a beleaguered police force at
least 10,000 men short.

In Brighton, of course, all this criminality was 'happily no more'
– or so the Preface to the Boultings' film would have us believe. As
if. On the day of *Brighton Rock*'s première, the Brighton *Evening Argus*
carried a report on an amusement arcade, a stone's throw from the
Savoy cinema, that a police spokesman described as 'a reception centre
for criminals'. In the same edition, an editorial warned of a 'crime wave'
that was 'growing in intensity'.[14] In reality, the South Coast resort was
something of a post-war haven for career criminals. Darby Sabini, the
leading race-course gangster, retired there and, according to his former
employee, 'Mad' Frankie Fraser, Brighton was 'an absolutely bent town'.
Its 'Guv'nor' was Sammy Bellson, a bookie and bar owner who owed
allegiance to Jack Spot and (later) Billy Hill.[15] In 1957, Bellson would
go on trial with the Chief Constable of Brighton and two of his officers
on charges relating to their dealings with bookmakers and club owners.
The Chief Constable escaped conviction with the others, but was obliged
to resign in disgrace. He had presided over a system of corruption
which, the trial revealed, dated back at least ten years, to the days of
Brighton Rock's filming.[16] Brighton's authorities may have cleared the
slums of Carlton Hill, but the corruption Greene had smelled in 1937
would linger on for the next two decades.

BRIGHTON ROCKED

What a disgrace to spivs! Surely something better than that could
have been made out of Graham Greene's best seller? Whoever heard

a good spiv say 'It isn't here' with the accent on the 'h'? [...] If this
is what the Boultings can do to portray spivs, I'm glad I registered last
Saturday. (Letter from 'Self-respecting Spiv' to the *Evening Argus*, 15
January 1948)

Unsurprisingly, the film's screening opened up a fierce debate in the local
press about the merits of its depictions of Brighton. The *Brighton and
Hove Herald* weighed in straightaway: '[T]here is a school of thought
which maintains that any publicity is good publicity. This film shows
the fallacy of that argument. It is true that there are some favourable
shots of Brighton's amenities; but Brighton is also shown as a town
of squalid slums, furtive slouching degenerates, and a place where the
police ignore evidence thrust under their noses.' Dismissing the film's
Preface as 'valueless', and condemning the picture as 'merely an essay
in brutality', the *Herald* chose to blame the authorities who had allowed
the town's facilities to be used for filming. They 'might at least have
read the novel on which the film is based and considered whether it
would be good publicity for Brighton'.[17]

Peter Black, the *Evening Argus* journalist referenced in the film's
mock-up newspaper report on Kite's death, took a diametrically opposed
view: 'It is an extremely well-made film; it is beautifully acted by a
hand-picked cast; the direction has captured unerringly the atmosphere
it sought – the rowdy, good-humoured fun of Brighton in sunshine,
contrasting with the squalor that between the wars lurked behind the
tall, blind buildings of its back streets.'[18]

One of those who had offered facilities for filming, the manager of
the Aquarium, lent his support to Black, endorsing the film's Preface and
arguing that 'this film will prove most useful publicity as it will bring
the name of the town before the British public, arousing curiosity in
those who have never spent a holiday here, and reminding the hundreds
of thousands who have that Brighton is still the Queen of the South
Coast'.[19]

Another letter-writer thought that the film could be used, with 'a
carefully-worded explanatory lecture', to teach the lesson that 'crime
does not pay'.[20] However, there were others who thought *Brighton Rock*
'a poor advertisement for Brighton', and could not understand why
the council had allowed 'such a bad and sordid film' to be exhibited
locally.[21] It was left to a former film exhibitor and producer to have
the last word in a debate that had raged for ten days. Condemning
Brighton Rock as 'a detestable film' he added: 'We want to put all this

trash behind us. Haven't two wars been grisly enough? Brighton, with its beautiful surroundings, is deserving of a better story and atmosphere on the films.'[22]

Controversy did no harm to the box-office takings. After a record-breaking first week, the Savoy's manager Alfred J. Sadler sent a telegram to the Boultings: 'Brighton demands a larger bite of *Brighton Rock*. Phenomenal success. All records rocking. Holding a further week.'[23] It was a similar story in London where *Brighton Rock*, opening on 9 January, broke all attendance records on its first two days at the Warner, Leicester Square. Sensing a box-office smash, Pathé extended the picture's release to the Dominion and New Victoria where it was held over for a second week, as it was on provincial pre-releases at Blackpool and Nottingham.[24] Box-office demand, *The Cinema* believed, was stoked by Reg Whitley's 'sensational outburst' and his warning about the horrific nature of the razor-slashing scenes.[25]

Whitley's condemnation was echoed more faintly by Leonard Mosley in the *Daily Express*. His '*Brighton Rock* doesn't taste right' contained the infamous description of Attenborough's Pinkie as 'about as close to the real thing as Donald Duck is to Greta Garbo'. Attenborough's 'gallant failure' in the part, combined with 'a slowness of pace', resulted in an overall feeling of disappointment that even 'the good shots of Brighton' could not dispel.[26] Mosley's colleague on the *Sunday Express*, Stephen Weeks, concurred, questioning the need for cinema to focus on razor gangs and regretting that the Boultings' adaptation lacked the depth of the novel with its 'mastery of the analysis of evil'.[27] Jack Davies in the *Sunday Graphic* was similarly unimpressed by Attenborough and, though the performances by Baddeley and Hartnell were strong, the film was not sufficiently his 'idea of fun' to recommend it to readers.[28] His belief that *Brighton Rock* was 'in every way a really well made picture, and yet cannot be classed as entertainment because its subject is sordid, squalid, sadistic and unpleasant' followed the dominant critical line and is revealing of the underlying assumptions and expectations of reviewers of the time. Elspeth Grant (*Daily Graphic*) and C. A. Lejeune (the *Observer*) were in full agreement.[29] Lejeune and Richard Winnington (*News Chronicle*) were particularly scandalised by the re-vised ending, describing it, respectively, as 'a thorough disgrace' and 'intensely displeasing'.[30] Their views were indicative of a widespread feeling that the book had not been done full justice. Paul Dehn (*Sunday Chronicle*) represented this line of criticism at its most developed when he complained that an 'unforgettable' novel had been turned into 'a very competent, capable and efficient thriller (no more)' by removing 95 per cent of the story's religious import.[31]

Although a critical consensus that cut across the political allegiances of newspapers emerged around the undesirability of its sordid subject matter and its dilution of the novel's religious themes, there were a few critics who were prepared to grant the Boultings' film relatively unqualified praise. Foremost among these was the *Daily Mail*'s Fred Majdalany, who pronounced the film 'good right through', finding it both more moving and more terrifying than similar offerings.[32] W. A. Wilcox (*Sunday Dispatch*) joined him in praising the acting and direction of what Wilcox called 'a masterly production of an exciting story'.[33] Wilcox was even prepared to challenge the critical orthodoxy by asking rhetorically: 'since when has it been honest for any form of art only to portray the sunnier and rosier side of life?' And in *Reynold's News*, Joan Lester detected 'the imprint of Boulting sincerity' in a well-made 'serious analysis of spivery'.[34]

Although *Brighton Rock* started its run like an express, it slowed a little as it did the rounds of provincial cinemas from the end of January.[35] It is clear, though, that *Brighton Rock* was one of ABPC's top grossing films of the 1940s. Board of Trade figures place it third behind *My Brother Jonathan* (1948) and *The Guinea Pig*, with a net revenue of £366,496 (almost double its production costs).[36] Robert Clark's studio accounts place it fourth after the two already mentioned and *The Hasty Heart* (1949), and this is corroborated by the statement of profit made to the studio by the distributors, Pathé.[37] This does not mean that ABPC actually made a profit on *Brighton Rock*. With a limited home market, most films (then as now) require effective international distribution to make them profitable. *Brighton Rock* proved particularly difficult to market abroad. Associated British were probably mindful of Whitley's well-publicised criticism that the film would spread an 'untrue picture of life in Britain'; and foreign exhibitors were wary of its theme. In Holland, for example, censors placed a ban on the film. Warner Bros' financial interest in Associated British might have been expected to ensure American distribution for a film that had been a hit in its home territory, but Associated British must have been apprehensive about the prospects of *Brighton Rock* running foul of the US Production Code Administration, not to mention vociferous Catholic and Jewish organisations. ABPC chose not to submit the film for consideration and Warners would not distribute an uncertificated picture. The film's release also coincided with the Dalton Duty crisis, during which Anglo-American relations were put under strain by the imposition of a swingeing duty on the importation of American movies. Consequently it took almost four years for *Brighton Rock* to gain an American release. Eventually, the Boultings struck a deal with a small outfit called Mayer-Kingsley to distribute *Brighton Rock* and their 1950 film, *Seven Days to Noon*. On 7 November 1951, Pinkie's exploits finally reached a Stateside screen on a very limited release, without a Production Code certificate, and under a title calculated to appeal to genre fans: *Young Scarface*.

LOOKING BACK FROM THE END OF THE PIER

The huge public has been trained to expect a villain and a hero, and if you think you're going to reach the biggest possible public, it's no good thinking of drama as a conflict of ideas; it's the conflict – in terms of sub-machine guns – between the plainest Good and the plainest Evil. (Graham Greene, 'Ideas in the Cinema', *Spectator*, 19 November 1937)

In the end, the film of *Brighton Rock* was overwhelmed by its times. Its subject matter was so pertinent to the dreams and fears of post-war social engineers that the film could never secure an artistic identity independent of political imperatives. The compromises and alternative priorities of film-making mean that no literary adaptation is entirely faithful to its source. At first sight, *Brighton Rock* might seem to have been approached with a greater fidelity than most, but its translation to the screen bears the subtle traces of a vision that was not the author's own, and a process of abridgement that was driven by the conventions of popular cinema rather than the need for greater understanding. For all that was gained – by the sullen intensity of Attenborough's performance, the support of his fellow actors, the shadowland created by Waxman's cinematography, and the sensitivity and fluidity of Boulting's direction – something was still lost.

What disappeared was Greene's pessimism, acceptable in the days of Hitler's rise and the economy's fall, but inappropriate to the project of post-war reconstruction. That stick of rock, Greene's symbol of the immutability of the human condition, hardly seemed suited to an age of progressive reform or, indeed, to the Boultings' conception of a more malleable social order. Perhaps, after all, the 'Worst Sin' – the sin of despair – might have been a title that more truly reflected their faith in social redemption through political action. *Nil desperandum* was an appropriate rallying cry for a world recovering from the trauma of total war, if not for Greene's dark cosmology. The film's Preface is easily dismissed as a sop to the local council, but perhaps it should also be seen, in the context of the times, as a wider exercise in wish fulfilment. The ante bellum conditions of *Brighton Rock*, if not exactly 'no more', were certainly the ones that had to be swept away by the zeal of reform. The Boultings would have endorsed the idea that if what was depicted in their film was not quite yet 'the world we have lost', then it was undoubtedly 'the world we must lose'. In this formulation, Pinkie can be seen as a personification of the evil of pre-war social inequality, nurtured in squalor and darkness and now exposed to the sunrays of enlightenment. Thus the prophetic Preface becomes a dramatic incantation, and the film itself a symbolic enactment in which evil is plucked from the heart of the community, consigned to the purifying waves, and is 'happily no more'. This might have been in keeping with Greene's penchant for the drama of the morality play, but not with his burning sense of the immortality of evil.

Ultimately, it is the Boultings' secular belief in social redemption through the efforts of resolute individuals and benevolent organisations, rather than Greene's religious faith in 'the appalling strangeness of the mercy of God', that is dominant in their film. A ministering nun and a final pan to a crucifix can only qualify the film's secularity. It is a grand gesture to the spirituality of the novel, but there is a triteness about it that critics were quick to spot. What fewer seemed to notice was the way in which *Brighton Rock*'s critique of social conditions had somehow been lost by film-makers one might have expected to take the utmost care in its conservation. If it was the ruthlessness of international capital that maintained the inequalities that bred Pinkie, and if it was philanthropy that cleared the slums and prevented a new generation of Pinkies, where is all this revealed in the film? What has become of its sociology? Richard Winnington was almost alone among reviewers in remarking that the film's criminal characters 'come from nowhere to flit motiveless before us. Pinkie is not explained. The hell that lay around him in his infancy and drives him from horror to horror is unexplained.'[38] For Greene, these social factors remained important enough for him, decades later, to comment: 'I don't think that Pinkie was guilty of mortal sin because his actions were not committed in defiance of God, but arose out of the conditions to which he had been born.'[39] Greene's screenplay had tried to incorporate some reference to the socio-political and psycho-sexual factors which, in the novel, are presented as contributing to Pinkie's delinquency; but his heart was no longer in secular understanding. As we have seen, his efforts, which the Boultings were happy to endorse, were finally negated by the editing process. The vestiges of a social explanation of Pinkie were stripped away and all that remained was evil. Instead of a damaged product of his environment, Pinkie became a psychopathic monster, a creature of supernatural malevolence for whom few could have sympathy. Out went the pathos of tragedy, leaving the less humanistic satisfactions of revenge and retribution. Consequently, Ida – a character who in the novel was primarily an incarnation of Pinkie's fate – was transformed into a righteous heroine carrying the weight of audience identification. Ironically, it was the socially idealistic Boultings who ultimately sanctioned the depoliticising of *Brighton Rock* and the reordering of its audience's sympathies; and equally ironically, the much maligned Preface is now all that remains of a sociological explanation of criminality. Greene's book had indicated that the children of the poor turn to violent crime as an expressive and economic release from a social situation in which they are allowed no control over their lives. Pinkie's need to break the cycle of family poverty gives him the courage to fight the fear of eternal damnation which inhibits his efforts. This message might have been appropriate for a literary readership in the winter of the 1930s depression, but it was largely 'unhelpful' in a film aimed at a mass audience in the spring of post-war reconstruction. In the midst of a crime wave that threatened the order on which reconstruction depended, what was required was not understanding but condemnation. Thus, at a cultural moment when the problems of crime and punishment loomed larger than the problems of poverty and unemployment, it is hardly surprising that the Boultings' film dispenses with Greene's tragic anti-hero and replaces him with a villain reeking of sulphur. Joan Lester in *Reynold's News* was impressed with the way in which the movie 'relentlessly deglamorises crime and the criminal', remarking, 'how completely authentic is the frustration and joylessness of these creatures, their fundamental cowardice!'[40]

As an intervention in the debate about juvenile delinquency, *Brighton Rock* was a salutary reminder of the enduring and intractable malevolence within the human spirit which the best therapeutic regimes find hard to treat. The film can almost be seen as a rejoinder to Jack Lee and Ian Dalrymple's little-seen paean to the possibilities of reforming social work, *Children on Trial* (1946). If it had followed the path of Greene's novel, the film might have been a powerful contribution to the liberal humanist arguments for penal reform advanced in the Criminal Justice Bill then passing through Parliament.[41] As it was, the Boultings' portrait of a teenage hoodlum compromised their own liberal consciences, fuelling fears of spivery and violent crime and, if anything, militating against the Bill's abolition of flogging and hard labour. Of course, films are so often less about the times in which they are set than about when they are made; and *Brighton Rock* now seems to say more about post-war anxieties than pre-war conditions. Shorn of his slum background, Pinkie can easily be taken for a child of the war rather than a hangover from the 1920s. He could easily represent a generation growing up without fathers, in shattered homes, with violence as an everyday reality. And it is difficult to view Ida now as anything other than a personification of the post-war assertive woman who challenges patriarchal power and provokes a repressive response: 'Won't anybody shut that brass's mouth?'

Fast-forward fifty years. It is 5 February 1999. Another Brighton audience sits in thrall while Attenborough, now a Knight of the silver screen, talks about the role that made him a star. Sussex University, where Lord Attenborough is Chancellor, is hosting a commemorative celebration of the film that has become as much a part of Brighton's cultural heritage as the Royal Pavilion. The invited audience includes Roy Boulting (the surviving twin) and a number of luminaries of British cinema. They clutch copies of the second *Brighton Rock* special edition to be published by the *Argus*, the paper that has remained loyal to the film over five decades. No one now questions whether Reg Whitley's 92 minutes of 'cheap, false, nasty sensationalism' was good for the resort, soon to take its place among Britain's cities. After all, the 'great and good' of Brit-film have just placed *Brighton Rock* at number 15 in the BFI's millennial poll of the nation's favourite movies, confirming Peter Graham Scott's belief that 'It was the best thing John [Boulting] did. It was ahead of the game, quite modern in its style and acting.'[42] As Britain has embraced its dark side, the Boultings' problem child has become a national treasure, a wonderful whiff of seaside 'orror, distinguished by a benchmark performance from Leicester's most distinguished son. Pinkie and Dickie, separated at birth, one finding his destiny on a pier, the other as a peer.

Now the millennium has turned and as we look back in the centenary year of Greene's birth, the tragedy of Pinkie Brown endures as a potent myth in our fallen world. In Thatcher's time, Pinkie's plea for someone to 'shut that brass's mouth' took on a new resonance, and in this latest age of New Labour, 'Greeneland', that gloomy realm of moral ambiguity and betrayal, has become the mental antidote to Blair-ite optimism. Pickled in brine and brimstone and swept back to shore on a fresh wave of British gangster cinema, Pinkie's remains are now carefully preserved: a shiny new print, two weeks of screenings at the Institute of Contemporary Arts, centrepiece of an exhibition of film visions of Brighton, a DVD release, resuscitation as a John Barry stage musical, and persistent reports of a remake by Terence Malik. Poor Reg Whitley must be revolving in his coffin; but it goes to show that, at least in the cinematic life eternal, mercy *may* be sought and found between the stirrup and the ground.

Notes

1. FILMING THE FALLEN WORLD

1. The Boultings' career is discussed in Alan Burton, Tim O'Sullivan and Paul Wells (eds), *The Family Way: The Boulting Brothers and British Film Culture* (Trowbridge: Flicks Books, 2000).

2. Harry Hopkins, *The New Look: A Social History of the Forties and Fifties* (London: Secker and Warburg, 1964), p. 91.

3. Ibid., p. 77.

4. For what remains one of the best articulations of Greene's pessimism, see Kenneth Allott and Miriam Farris, *The Art of Graham Greene* (London: Hamish Hamilton, 1951).

5. Graham Greene, *The Heart of the Matter* (London: Heinemann, 1948).

6. Graham Greene, *Brighton Rock* (London: Heinemann, 1938), p. 226. Page numbers refer to the current Penguin edition.

7. Elizabeth Sewell, 'Graham Greene', *Dublin Review*, vol. 228, no. 463 (1954): 12–24.

8. Graham Greene, *British Dramatists* (London: Collins, 1942).

9. Greene, *The Heart of the Matter*.

10. John Atkins, *Graham Greene* (London: John Calder, 1957), p. 95.

11. Norman Sherry, *The Life of Graham Greene: Volume One: 1904–1939* (London: Penguin, 1990), pp. 92–9.

12. Frank Krutnik, *In a Lonely Street: Film Noir, Genre, Masculinity* (London: Routledge, 1991).

13. The wonder is that so few critics have been led down the trail. Most literary commentators seem blind to the possibilities of a psychoanalytic reading.

14. Raymond Durgnat, 'Some Lines of Inquiry into Post-war British Crimes', in Robert Murphy (ed.), *The British Cinema Book*, 2nd edn (London: BFI, 2002), p. 136.

15. Thus, although Burton et al. (*The Family Way*, p. 10) are describing the comedies of the 1950s when they identify the Boultings' fundamental theme as 'the reconstruction of the "individual" within unstable and sometimes anachronistic determinations of "society"', it really begins with *Brighton Rock*.

16. John Hill, *Sex, Class and Realism: British Cinema 1956–63* (London: BFI, 1986), p. 147.

17. John Boulting in Colin Belfrage, *All is Grist* (London: Parallax Press, 1988), p. 164.

18. Sidney Bernstein, *Film and International Relations* (London: Workers' Film Association, 1945).

19. Discussions of the 'Spiv' cycle include: Robert Murphy, *Realism and Tinsel* (London: Routledge, 1989), Ch. 8; Peter Wollen, 'Riff-raff Realism', *Sight & Sound*, April 1998; Tim Pulleine, 'Spin a Dark Web', in Steve Chibnall and Robert Murphy (eds), *British Crime Cinema* (London: Routledge, 1999), pp. 27–36. The cycle was accompanied by an explosion of English hard-boiled pulp novels that caused considerable concern to the authorities.

20. Robert Warshow, 'The Gangster as Tragic Hero', *Partisan Review*, February 1948.

21. John K. Walton, *The British Seaside* (Manchester: Manchester University Press, 2000).

22. Michael Balcon, *Realism or Tinsel?* (London: Workers' Film Association, 1944).

23. Graham Greene, *Ways of Escape* (London: Penguin, 1980), p. 61.

24. Roy Boulting, conversation with the author, Brighton, 5 February 1999.

25. These contradictions are discussed in Frank Gray, Steve Chibnall and Andy Medhurst, *Kiss and Kill: Film Visions of Brighton* (Brighton and Hove: Royal Pavilion Libraries and Museums, 2002).

26. '[I]n truth these sordid undercurrents of life in Brighton were very largely confined to the race-course and to a few public houses, dance halls, amusement arcades and cafes in a very restricted quarter of town, and the majority of residents and visitors were quite unaware of these disturbances below the surface' (Clifford Musgrave, *Life in Brighton*, Rochester: John Hallewell, 1981), p. 387.

27. Michael Sheldon, *Graham Greene: The Man Within* (London: Heinemann, 1994).

28. Greene, *Brighton Rock*, p. 140.

29. Ibid., p. 142. As Martin Rubin has argued, 'a strong sense of *contrast* between two different dimensions' is a 'crucial condition' for the thriller (*Thrillers*, Cambridge: Cambridge University Press, 1999), p. 17.

30. *Brighton Gazette*, 3 September 1938.

31. Patrick Hamilton, *Hangover Square* (London: Penguin, 1974), p. 166.

32. Charles Drazin, *The Finest Years* (London: André Deutsch, 1998), p. 76.

33. *Evening Standard*, 30 November 1945.

34. *News Chronicle*, 1 December 1945.

35. Frankie Fraser, *Mad Frank's Diary* (London: Virgin, 2001), p. 89.

36. Robert Murphy, *Smash and Grab* (London: Faber, 1993), pp. 27–9.

37. Frankie Fraser, *Mad Frank* (London: Warner Books, 1995), p. 13.

38. R. Samuel, *East End Underworld* (London: Routledge, 1981), p. 183.

39. Ibid., p. 184.

40. Wensley Clarkson, *Hit 'em Hard: Jack Spot, King of the Underworld* (London: HarperCollins, 2002), p. 47.

41. One of Hill's friends recalled: 'He kept control with the razor. People were paid a pound a stitch, so if you put twenty stitches in a man you got a score. You used to look in the evening papers the next day to see how much you'd earned' (James Morton, *Gangland: London's Underworld*, London: Warner Books, 1993), p. 46.

42. Ibid., pp. 42–5. For a contemporary account of the race gangs, see W. Bebbington, *Rogues Go Racing* (London: Good and Benn, 1947). See also, Mike Huggins, *Horseracing and the British* (Manchester: Manchester University Press, 2003), pp. 145–50.

2. PLANNING AND EXECUTION

1. Interviewed by Mort Rosenblum, *St Louis Post Dispatch*, 12 September 1982.

2. *The Times*, 27 July 1939, p. 12. Born in 1912, Frank Harvey entered the theatre after studying English at Cambridge. *Saloon Bar* (filmed in 1940) was his first major success as a writer. He worked on the adaptation of *Brighton Rock* before his military service in the Royal Tank Corps. Wounded at El Alamein, he was posted to the Army Film Unit at Pinewood where he worked on documentaries such as *Burma Victory* (1945) and probably first encountered the Boulting brothers. He went on to script some of their best films, including *Seven Days to Noon* (1950), *Private's Progress* (1957) and *I'm All Right, Jack* (1959). Harvey died in 1981.

3. Pinkie, Greene believed, should be played by 'a youth who can look neurotic and seventeen and sinister' and Rose by someone very young 'and not at all glamorous' (Norman Sherry, *The Life of Graham Greene: Volume Two*, London: Penguin, 1996), p. 160.

4. Ibid., p. 162.

5. *The Times*, 17 February 1966, p. 15.

6. A fragment of what may have been the draft that Greene approved in 1940, held in Brighton's reference library, includes a priest in its *dramatis personae*, and a fourth scene in Act Three set in Pinkie's room. However, a comparison with the programme for the Garrick production reveals that no priest is listed among the characters, and that Act Three ended with Scene Three on the Palace Pier. This is confirmed by *Theatre World*'s photographs of the production, the last of which is set on the pier. The caption gives a positive spin to the ending: 'Ida tries to comfort the hysterical Rose, who clings desperately to the tell-tale record of Pinkie's voice; the record that will fortunately, we feel sure, shatter for ever the love she bore him' (*Theatre World*, April 1943, pp. 9–20).

7. Sherry, *The Life of Graham Greene: Volume Two*, pp. 163–4.

8. *Picture Post*, 20 March 1943, p. 11.

9. *Picture Post* hinted at what had befallen Greene's allegorical text: 'Theatrical convention, in fact, has turned the book into something like a conventional thriller' (ibid.).

10. Sherry, *The Life of Graham Greene: Volume Two*, p. 164.

11. Geoffrey Wansell, *Terence Rattigan: A Biography* (London: Fourth Estate, 1995), p. 96.

12. Included in a letter from A. D. Peters to Rattigan on 7 January 1947. Sir Terence Rattigan Collection at the British Library.

13. Robert Stannage, *Stars by Day* (London: Ward and Hitchon, 1947), p. 79.

14. *Brighton Argus Brighton Rock Special*, 5 February 1999.

15. Ibid.

16. Quentin Falk, *Travels in Greeneland*, 3rd edn (London: Reynolds and Hearn, 2000) p. 42; letter from Rattigan to John Boulting, 11 October 1946 (Rattigan Collection).

17. *Argus Brighton Rock Special*. Greene's worst experience of scripting was on his adaptation of John Galsworthy's *Twenty-One Days* (Basil Dean, 1939).

18. Board of Trade figures place the final cost at £192,436, but this probably includes some promotional expenditure (Philip Gillett, *The British Working Class in PostwarFilm*, Manchester: Manchester University Press, 2003), p. 201.

19. £12,000 must be considered a bargain in the context of the £37,500 paid in the same year by Korda for the screen rights to Rattigan's play *The Winslow Boy*, which was first performed in Brighton in February 1946 (Wansell, *Terence Rattigan*, pp. 158, 161).

20. Rattigan Collection. A fifty-nine-page hand-written original also survives.

21. *The Spectator*, 27 October 1939.

22. One of biographer Norman Sherry's informants indicated that Greene disliked Rattigan, not simply for his homosexuality, but because he made a secret of it, maintaining the varnish of respectability (Sherry, *The Life of Graham Greene: Volume Two*, p. 248).

23. Interview with Gene D. Phillips, S.J., *The Catholic World*, August 1969, pp. 218–21.

24. Interview with Quentin Falk, National Film Theatre, 3 September 1984.

25. Interviewed in Brian McFarlane, *An Autobiography of British Cinema* (London: BFI/Methuen, 1997), p. 34.

26. Republished in David Parkinson (ed.), *Mornings in the Dark: The Graham Greene Film Reader* (London: Penguin, 1995), pp. 418–20.

27. Graham Greene, *Second Treatment for Brighton Rock*, Rattigan Collection.

28. Graham Greene, 'Subjects and Stories', in Charles Davy (ed.), *Footnotes to the Film* (London: Lovat Dickson, 1938).

29. *The Spectator*, 14 August 1936.

30. Rattigan Collection.

31. *The Cinema*, 12 March 1947.

32. *The Spectator*, 6 December 1935. On the other hand, he was conscious of 'how seldom in English films a director uses the camera in this way to establish a scene, a way of life, with which he and his audience are familiar'.

33. *The Spectator*, 21 April 1939. The choice of the final word 'battlefields' is a mark of his identification with Woods's film. Greene's own book *It's a Battlefield* (1934) shares some of the same themes.

34. 'If you are using words in one craft,' he once wrote, 'it is impossible not to corrupt them by employing them in another medium' ('The Novelist and the Cinema: A Personal Experience', in William Whitebait [ed.], *International Film Annual*, New York: Doubleday, 1958).

35. *The Spectator*, 11 December 1936.

36. *The Spectator*, 16 June 1939.

37. Interview with Falk, op. cit. Greene's comment, in the same interview, that Carol Reed was 'the only director' with whom he had enjoyed working, suggests a lack of rapport with the Boultings.

38. Interviewed in McFarlane, *An Autobiography of British Cinema*, p. 78.

39. *The Cinema*, 12 March 1947.

40. *Argus Brighton Rock Special*, p. 4.

41. Ibid.

42. McFarlane, *An Autobiography of British Cinema*, p. 79.

43. James Robertson cites the case of *The Saint in London* (1939) as evidence of this softening attitude ('The Censors and British Gangland 1913–1990', in Steve Chibnall and Robert Murphy [eds], *British Crime Cinema*, London: Routledge, 1999), p. 16.

44. Ibid., pp. 17–18.

45. Ibid., p. 18.

46. *The Spectator*, 14 August 1936.

47. *Daily Mirror*, 9 January 1948.

48. *Third Time Lucky* Exploitation Folder, Alliance-Anglofilm, London, 1948.

49. Gillett, *The British Working Class in Postwar Film*, p. 108. Compare, for example, Attenborough's suit with similar styles worn by John Mills and Robert Newton in *The Green Cockatoo* (1938). Plesch's designs are discussed in *The Worst Sin* pressbook, Associated British Pathé, 1947. The designer would eventually run a jewellery shop at the end of Brighton's Palace Pier.

50. Peter Graham Scott, interview with the author, 17 November 2003.

51. *The Worst Sin* pressbook.

52. Compare it, for example, with Visconti's *Ossessione* (1943) and *La Terra Trema* (1948).

53. *The Cinema*, 22 January 1947.

54. *Argus Brighton Rock Special*, p. 8.

55. Lord Attenborough, interviewed in McFarlane, *An Autobiography of British Cinema*, p. 34.

56. Lord Attenborough, interviewed in *The Many Lives of Richard Attenborough*, BBC2, 24 May 2003.

57. *The Cinema*, 12 March 1947; Stannage, *Stars by Day*, p. 80.

58. *The Worst Sin* pressbook.

59. The hot lights allowed Carol to come through the freezing shoot relatively unscathed. The photographer succumbed to bronchitis (*The Cinema*, 5 March 1947).

60. Ibid.

61. *The Cinema*, 19 March 1947. To maintain the enthusiasm of the unit, Waxman hung blown-up 35mm prints of recent filming on a display board on one side of the studio.

62. *The Cinema*, 26 March 1947.

63. *Home Review*, November 1947, p. 14.

64. Ibid. An earlier account suggested that things had not gone quite so smoothly. A fragment of grit had lodged in one of Marsh's eyes, and had to be removed by a doctor. *Film-Shot*, vol. 2, no. 2, May 1947: 11.

65. *Brighton Argus Brighton Rock Special*, p. 6.

66. Ibid.

67. *The Cinema*, 26 May 1947.

68. *Film-Shot*, vol. 2, no. 2, May 1947: p. 12.

69. *The Cinema*, 23 and 30 April 1947. The Grosvenor and Savoy Hotels lent page boys for the shoot.

70. *The Cinema*, 7 May 1947.

71. Sally is featured in Robert Stannage's account of his visit to the set: 'For some time, Sally was a great admirer of "Uncle" Dickie Attenborough. But when she saw "Dickie" (in his part as the despicable "Pinkie", of course) reclining on a dishevelled bed in a tenement house, plucking the hairs from a doll's head, poor little Sally could not conceal her dismay. Now her eyes do not light up whenever Attenborough is around!' (*Stars by Day*, p. 79).

72. *The Cinema*, 7 May 1947.

73. Ibid.

74. *The Cinema*, 14, 21 and 28 May 1947.

75. *The Cinema*, 21 May 1947.

76. Ibid.

77. *The Cinema*, 28 May 1947.

78. *The Cinema*, 4 June 1947.

79. *The Cinema*, 11 June 1947.

80. *The Cinema*, 18 June 1947.

81. *The Cinema*, 25 June 1947.

82. Constance Smith deserves a book of her own. Like Rose, the beautiful Irish actress was born into poverty. By the time she was twenty-three she had graduated from telephonist to Hollywood starlet in films such as *The 13th Letter* (1951) and *Red Skies of Montana* (1952), before sinking back into poverty in Rome in the late 1950s. Her emotional life was the stuff of grand opera: once married to Bryan Forbes, she became the lover of Paul Rotha, whom she tried to kill on two occasions. Periods of prison and treatment followed, before she finally disappeared after discharging herself from a Lewisham hospital (see *Classic Images*, 216, June 1993: 40–1, 44; and Bryan Forbes, *Notes for a Life*, London: Everest Books, 1977, pp. 205–14).

83. *The Cinema*, 9 July 1947.

84. *The Cinema*, 16 July 1947.

85. *The Cinema*, 23 July 1947. Special permission to break austerity regulations and keep the pier lights on throughout the night had been obtained from the Ministry of Fuel and Power.

86. W. J. West, *The Quest for Graham Greene* (London: Weidenfeld and Nicolson, 1997), p. 123.

87. *Brighton and Hove Gazette*, 1 February 1984.

88. Brighton *Evening Argus*, 25 July 1947.

89. *The Cinema*, 30 July 1947. Rival resort Eastbourne quickly stepped in with the offer of facilities. A full account can be found in the *Brighton Herald*, 2 August 1947.

90. Attenborough, interviewed by Frank Gray, 9 July 2001 (*Kiss and Kill Catalogue*).

91. *Brighton Herald*, 2 August 1947.

92. These additional shots were filmed at Welwyn and Harpenden early in September (*The Cinema*, 10 September 1947).

93. *The Cinema*, 13 August 1947.

94. *Brighton Herald*, 9 August 1947.

95. *The Cinema*, 20 August 1947.

96. *The Cinema*, 27 August 1947. Most of the 200 scene stills, 200 publicity stills, 60 portraits, 130 character portraits and 25 fashion stills survive in the archive of Canal + Image UK.

97. See *The Cinema*, 21 November 1947 and *Kinematograph Weekly*, 20 November 1947.

3. IN THE CAN

1. Used as a code by Wormold in Greene's *Our Man in Havana*.

2. See the opening credits of the crime melodrama *Jump for Glory* (1938), for example.

3. The paper suggests that it is the summer of 1935, although the publicity for the film maintains that it is set in 1937, the year in which the book was written.

4. 'I was doing the races then. Kite had a rival gang. [...] He'd tried to bump my boss off on the course. Half of us took a fast car back to town. He thought we were on the train with him. But we were on the platform, see, when the train came in. We got round him directly he got outside the carriage. I cut his throat and the others held him up till we were all through the barrier in a bunch. Then we dropped him by the bookstall and did a bolt' (Graham Greene, *A Gun for Sale* [1936] London: Penguin, 1972 edn, p. 130). The date on the newspaper would fit the timeframe of *A Gun for Sale*.

5. At least the newspaper does not suggest that Kite was killed by Pinkie Brown as W. J. West mistakenly does in his *The Quest for Graham Greene* (London: Weidenfeld and Nicolson, 1997), p. 78. Sometimes it might be better if Greene scholars paid less attention to the author's life and more to his writing.

6. Greene, himself, was not immune to the attractions of teenage boys, and Michael Sheldon suggests that he probably indulged his tastes during some visits to the Mediterranean (Sheldon, *Graham Greene: The Man Within*, London: Heinemann, 1994, p. 81).

7. Nelson Place is actually Rose's home in the novel. Pinkie is said to come from another part of the slum, Paradise Piece, suggesting his status as a fallen angel.

8. One of these photographs actually appeared in World Films Publications' annual *Preview*, published in November 1947 (p. 57). The caption reads: 'A Brighton gang discuss the death of their leader'.

9. The decision to set the first scene on Brighton station conforms to Rattigan's original treatment, which also introduces the idea of two female Kolley Kibber hunters.

10. A production still relating to this sequence is reproduced in Maire McQueeney, *The Brighton Rock Picture Book* (Brighton: Dining Table Publications, 1999), p. 47. The sequence is described in Robert Stannage, *Stars by Day* (London: Ward and Hitchon, 1947) p. 78. Stannage's claim that the bookstall had been stocked with period (1937) books and magazines is unfortunately discredited by a close shot that reveals that the novelettes are from the 1940s rather than the '30s.

11. Andrew Spicer, *Typical Men* (London: I.B. Tauris, 2001), Ch. 7. Greene once commented: 'I had spent only one night in the company of someone who could have belonged to Pinkie's gang – a man from the Wandsworth dog-tracks whose face had been carved because he was suspected of grassing to the bogies after a killing at the stadium' (*Ways of Escape*, London: Penguin, 1980, p. 61).

12. A further transitional sequence, covering four camera set-ups, also failed to make the final cut. It followed Dallow as he climbed the stairs and knocked at Pinkie's door, and included a high angle reaction shot of Frank, Judy and Cubitt, a still of which is preserved in Canal + collection. Shooting script, set-up 16.

13. Greene had singled out this innovation for praise, at the time, in a letter (4 March 1943) to his agent Laurence Pollinger and incorporated it into his screenplay (Norman Sherry, *The Life of Graham Green: Volume Two*, London: Penguin, 1996, p. 164).

14. The pub Greene had in mind for this scene is thought to be the Star and Garter (later Dr Brighton's) adjacent to Brighton's Savoy cinema where the film premièred (Norman Sherry, *The Life of Graham Greene: Volume One: 1904–1939*, London: Penguin, 1990, p. 632).

15. The trams were discontinued in 1939, but their wires are still visible above Queens Road. In a rare lapse of continuity, the no. 40 bus Fred boards becomes a no. 6 in the next shot.

16. McQueeney, *The Brighton Rock Picture Book*, pp. 4, 7, 10, 36, 37.

17. In the novel, Fred searches the seafront, rather than the pier, for a pick-up.

18. Joan Sterndale-Bennett was the daughter of entertainer Thomas Case Sterndale and began her stage career in 1933. It included a long association with the Players Theatre, and ended in 1970 with the farce *No Sex Please, We're British*. She had a number of character parts in films, including *We Dive at Dawn* (1943) and *Tawny Pipit*.

19. *Brighton Rock*, p. 15.

20. In his film treatment, Rattigan had renamed the horse Satan's Colt. He has Fred tell Ida that, yes, he believes in Satan, to which she responds, 'Well anyway, Satan had better win on Saturday, or else', and makes a playful gesture of slitting his throat.

21. Greene, quoted in Sherry, *The Life of Graham Greene: Volume Two*, p. 163.

22. '[A] touch of the nursery and the mother, stole from the big tipsy mouth, the magnificent breasts and legs … ' (*Brighton Rock*, p. 17).

23. See, for example, Sheldon, *Graham Greene: The Man Within*, p. 235. The principal evidence is Cubitt's remark that he 'can't see a piece of Brighton rock without … ' remembering Fred's murder. The other cryptic reference comes from Pinkie when he offers Rose a choice between winkles and rock. When she chooses the stick of rock, he thinks that 'only the devil […] could have made her answer like that' (*Brighton Rock*, pp. 162, 178).

24. The Palace Pier ghost train was the site of a real fire in 2002.

25. Peter Wollen, 'Riff-raff Realism', *Sight & Sound*, April 1998, p. 20.

26. The screams are a prime example of the film's attention to detail. Frank McNally, and Peter Graham Scott, recorded over 100 feet of shrieks from forty participants. Scott was also responsible for tipping a camera off the Palace Pier to simulate Fred's fall (*Today's Cinema*, 9 July 1947; McQueeney, *The Brighton Rock Picture Book*, p. 19).

27. The participation of two other members in the surveillance of Fred indicates that the gang numbers at least six.

28. Snow's may have been modelled on the Swan Café and Restaurant, close to where filming took place on King's Road (Seafront).

29. Stone probably had more roles in British films than any other actor during a career of almost forty years. A prize-winning student at RADA, she was discovered by Betty Box and cast in *When the Bough Breaks* (1947). Although she has precious few lines in *Brighton Rock*, John Boulting described her as 'one of the cleverest young actresses who has ever worked for me' (*Cinema Studio*, September 1950). His exaggerated praise may have been designed to impress her husband, the ubiquitous film critic Peter Noble. Stone and Carol Marsh reprised their roles as waitresses in Betty Box's 1949 film *Marry Me*, directed by Terence Fisher.

30. *Brighton Rock*, p. 28.

31. Leonard Goldman, *Oh What a Lovely Shore* (1996), p. 78. Note, too, the similarity of Ouida and ouija (board).

32. The Russell Square location is one of a number of references in the novel to T.S. Eliot, whose publisher's offices were situated there. For a reason not yet understood, Greene repeatedly used variations on the name 'Crow' in association with the victims of murderous violence.

33. Sheldon, *Graham Green: The Man Within*, pp. 246–7.

34. Bottles of vitriol were common weapons among the race gangs according to ex-Superintendent Fred Narborough, *Murder on My Mind* (London: Allan Wingate, 1959), p. 36.

35. McQueeney, *The Brighton Rock Picture Book*, p. 18.

36. *Brighton Rock*, p. 50. On the significance of dance halls in the films of the period see Philip Gillett, *The British Working Class in Postwar Film* (Manchester: Manchester University Press, 2003), Ch. 9.

37. The novel reveals that Rose lies about her age. She is sixteen, not seventeen (*Brighton Rock*, p. 74)

38. Ibid., p. 49.

39. Shooting script set-ups 149 and 151.

40. Quoted in Robert Murphy, *Smash and Grab* (London: Faber, 1993), p. 31.

41. The Cosmopolitan is based on Brighton's Bedford Hotel which was destroyed by a fire in the 1960s.

42. He is momentarily distracted by the paging of a Mr Al Parker, Attenborough's agent.

43. It is easy to see a parallel between Pinkie's interview with Colleoni and Greene's own first meeting with Korda which took place in November 1936 while *Brighton Rock* was being written.

44. '[H]e looked as a man might look who owned the whole world, the whole visible world, that is: the cash registers and policemen and prostitutes, Parliament and the laws which say "this is Right and this is Wrong"' (*Brighton Rock*, p. 65).

45. Shooting script, set-up 210.

46. It was while performing at this venue that Max Miller was 'discovered'. For a history of pierrots and concert parties, see Bill Pertwee, *Pertwee's Promenades*

and Pierrots: One Hundred Years of Seaside Entertainment (Newton Abbot: David and Charles, 1979).

47. Those familiar with Greene's film criticism might be reminded of his comments on Lily Pons in *I Dream Too Much* (John Cromwell, 1936): 'Nor have American directors learnt how ugly the close up of a woman singing must inevitably be: we are treated to many dreadful shots of a cavernous mouth projecting high notes like shells from a trench mortar' (*The Spectator*, 21 February 1936). The pierrots' song was written by the film's production manager Gerry Bryant.

48. A report in *The Cinema*, 30 July 1947, suggests that this scene was actually filmed, but there is no corroborating production still in the Canal + Images collection, and Peter Graham Scott cannot definitely recall the scene.

49. Shooting script, set-up 265. The dialogue is adapted from the conversation that takes place in the novel during Pinkie and Rose's trip to Peacehaven. Rattigan's treatment sets his version of the scene on the pier.

50. Ibid.

51. As the novel makes clear, Pinkie knew Nelson Place well: 'he could have drawn its plan as accurately as a surveyor on the turf: the barred and battlemented Salvation Army gaff at the corner: his own home beyond in Paradise Piece: the houses which looked as if they had passed through an intensive bombardment, flapping gutters and glassless windows, an iron bedstead rusting in the front garden, the smashed and wasted ground in front where houses had been pulled down for model flats which had never gone up (*Brighton Rock*, p. 90). For an account of life on Carlton Hill in the 1920s and 1930s see Robert Hayward, *Little to Spare and Nothing to Waste* (Brighton: Brighton Books, 1998).

52. The quotation is from a poem by William Camden (1551–1623).

53. Interview with the author.

54. The pin-ups of horses above his bed anticipate the next scene at the racecourse.

55. Spicer's declaration that Nottingham would be a good place to go is a reference to Greene's conversion to Roman Catholicism while working in the city. Ironically, Nottingham is also Raven's destination after the murder of Kite in *A Gun for Sale*.

56. We should have seen Pinkie replace the receiver and go upstairs 'chanting softly to himself *Agnus Dei qui tollis peccata mundi*', but again this reference to the Mass was deemed inappropriate by the BBFC.

57. *Brighton Rock*, p. 106.

58. Ibid., p. 113.

59. Set-ups 313–16.

60. Just as we saw the menacing shadows of Pinkie and Dallow through the glass of Brewer's door.

61. Set-up 330.

62. Greene's original 'God damn you, you little bitch', was softened only slightly to accommodate the censor.

63. Greene describes the film: 'magnificent features, thighs shot with studied care, esoteric beds shaped like winged coracles. A man was killed, but that didn't matter. What mattered was the game. The two main characters made their stately progress towards the bed-sheets' (*Brighton Rock*, p. 179). George Orwell might have had Pinkie's courtship in mind when he condemned the 'anonymous life of the dancehalls and the false values of the American film' in his 1946 essay 'Decline of the English Murder', in *Collected Essays and Journalism, Vol. 4* (London: Penguin, 1971), p. 128.

64. Ida's maternal nature is subtly indicated when she prevents Corkery from pouring his own tea.

65. For a discussion of the negative representation of love and marriage in 1940s *noir*, see Sylvia Harvey, 'Woman's Place: The Absent Family of Film *Noir*', in E. Ann Kaplan (ed.), *Women in Film Noir* (London: BFI, 1978), pp. 23–5.

66. Cubitt's doll was another Rattigan suggestion.

67. The phrase Dallow uses to calm Cubitt, 'he's lakes', is rhyming slang for 'barmy' (Lakes of Killarney).

68. In the novel, Prewitt confesses to an urge to expose himself in a park (*Brighton Rock*, p. 211).

69. Appropriately, the tune playing is 'You're Driving Me Crazy'.

70. Her descent was the production's first footage of Baddeley.

71. Nigel Richardson has made a plausible case for the trope of the suicide pact being inspired by an actual case in Brighton's Brunswick Terrace in October 1936. A middle-aged man had tried to make the murder of a younger homo-sexual lover look like a double suicide and, though found guilty of murder, had been reprieved: 'I remember reading in the papers ... He didn't hang' (Richardson, *Breakfast in Brighton*, London: Gollancz, 1998, pp. 164–8).

72. The sharp-eyed might spot continuity problems involving Ida's hat in this and her previous two scenes.

73. For a discussion of the relationship between the 'stranger' and the city, see the introduction to David B. Clarke (ed.), *The Cinematic City* (London: Routledge, 1997), p. 4.

74. In the absence of the deleted previous scene, their arrival is unmotivated. In another change to the shooting script, Corkery tries to indicate to the barman that he and Ida have arrived together by accident, suggesting that he is probably a married man trying to keep his affair secret. Small details like this add depth to the film's characters.

75. Wollen, 'Riff-raff Realism', p. 22.

76. 'Glory' is an important concept in Greene's fiction. The Glory of Sin entails the isolation of the individual from God and humanity, and the preparedness to transgress every sacred and secular rule in a 'rage of personality'.

77. *Brighton Rock*, p. 239.

78. In the shooting script, the close-up of the crucifix also opens the scene (set-up 522).

79. Rattigan, *First Treatment of Brighton Rock*, Rattigan Collection.

80. Roy Boulting, interviewed in *Empire of the Censors*, BBC2, May 1995. See also his interview in the *Argus Brighton Rock Special*, p. 5.

81. John Boulting, interviewed 7 October 1970. Judith Adamson, *Graham Greene and Cinema* (Norman, OK: Pilgrim Books, 1984), p. 41.

82. 'I thought it was so corny at the end of a film that had been so real' (Peter Graham Scott, interview with the author).

83. Adamson, *Graham Greene and Cinema*, p. 41.

84. Graham Greene, 'Introduction', *The Third Man and The Fallen Idol* (London: Heinemann, 1950), pp. 5–6.

85. Graham Greene, interviewed by Gene D. Phillips, op. cit.

86. Adamson, *Graham Greene and Cinema*, p. 41.

4. RELEASE

1. Brighton *Evening Argus*, 9 January 1948.

2. *The Cinema*, 14 January 1948.

3. *The Cinema*, 26 November 1947.

4. *Kinematograph Weekly*, 27 November 1947.

5. *The Cinema*, 17 December 1947.

6. Reg Whitley, 'False, Nasty: Is This What You Want to See', *Daily Mirror*, 9 January 1948.

7. 'Razor-Slasher Film is Defended by the Man Who Wrote the Book', *Daily Mirror*, 9 January 1948.

8. *Evening Standard*, 8 January 1948.

9. *Evening News*, 8 January 1948.

10. *The Cinema*, 24 December 1947.

11. *The Cinema*, 6 January 1948.

12. Geoffrey Webb (ed. Neil Tuson), *The Inside Story of Dick Barton* (London: Convoy Publications, 1950).

13. John Boulting, quoted in Robert Stannage, *Stars by Day* (London: Ward and Hitchon, 1947), p. 79.

14. *Evening Argus*, 8 January 1948. Crime statistics for Brighton in 1947 were as follows: crimes reported 2,140. Breaking and entering 490 (50 per cent increase on previous year). Thefts from unattended cars 114. One rape, two murders and two attempted murders. Crimes by juveniles decreased from 296 in 1946 to 182 (*Evening Argus*, 17 January 1948).

15. Frankie Fraser, *Mad Frank* (London: Warner Books, 1995), pp. 119–20.

16. For accounts of the Brighton police scandal see James Morton, *Bent Coppers* (London: Warner Books, 1994), pp. 95–102; Michael Connor, *The Soho Don* (London: Mainstream, 2002), pp. 13–29, 75–7.

17. *Brighton and Hove Herald*, 10 January 1948.

18. *Evening Argus*, 13 January 1948.

19. Letter from K. F. Moorhouse, *Evening Argus*, 14 January 1948.

20. Letter from Eric Mason, *Evening Argus*, 16 January 1948.

21. Letter from 'Filmgoer', *Evening Argus*, 16 January 1948.

22. Letter from P. Edwin Paterson, *Evening Argus*, 19 January 1948.

23. *The Cinema*, 28 January 1948. *Brighton Rock* was also showing at the Granada, Hove. In both runs it played with *Scrapbook for 1922* and a full supporting programme.

24. *The Cinema*, 23 January 1948.

25. *The Cinema*, 14 January 1948.

26. *Daily Express*, 9 January 1948.

27. *Sunday Express*, 11 January 1948.

28. *Sunday Graphic*, 11 January 1948.

29. *Daily Graphic*, 9 January 1948; *Observer*, 11 January 1948.

30. *News Chronicle*, 10 January 1948.

31. *Sunday Chronicle*, 11 January 1948.

32. *Daily Mail*, 9 January 1948.

33. *Sunday Dispatch*, 11 January 1948.

34. *Reynold's News*, 11 January 1948.

35. The film may have performed better in the south of England than in the north; but a comparison of the calculations made by Philip Gillett of the number of screenings of films in south-east Essex and in working-class cinemas in Leeds, reveals less variation than might have been anticipated. *Brighton Rock* is placed in mid-table in each locality (*The British Working Class in Postwar Film*, Manchester: Manchester University Press, 2003, pp. 203–4).

36. Ibid., p. 201.

37. Vincent Porter, 'The Robert Clark Account', *Historical Journal of Film, Radio and Television*, vol. 20, no. 4, October 2000: 469–511.

38. *News Chronicle*, 10 January 1948. *The Times*'s critic also thought the lack of an explanation of Pinkie a serious flaw: 'The influences that went to make him hate life with the passion the normal reserve for love, his preoccupation with hell and damnation, his twisted Catholicism, are either omitted or merely hinted at' (12 January 1948).

39. Marie-Françoise Allain, *The Other Man: Conversations with Graham Greene* (London: Bodley Head, 1983), pp. 158–9.

40. *Reynold's News*, 11 January 1948.

41. The Criminal Justice Act (1948) abolished hard labour, penal servitude and flogging, and created new provisions for preventative detention and corrective training. The Act provided a focus for contradictory discourses of social discipline and therapy. Old Testament ideas of retribution, revenge and

awful deterrence were challenged by New Testament notions of reform and forgiveness.

42. Interview with the author.

QM LIBRARY
(MILE END)